Dealing with Feelings

What this book is about

This is a book about using stories to help children's personal, social and emotional development.

Problem and challenging behaviour – in adults as well as in children – can often be traced to an individual's difficulties in processing and coming to terms with their own emotions, in communicating them, or in understanding other people's. The ability to do these things has been termed emotional intelligence. In 2003 Hovingham Primary School introduced an initiative to encourage the development of emotional intelligence, or 'emotional literacy', as the school prefers to call it. Central to this was an approach through stories and literature. This book presents an account of that work written by Jane Fisher, the teacher responsible.

The book is in three sections: the first explores what emotional literacy is and why it is important; the second gives an account of how stories were harnessed at Hovingham to help children develop emotional literacy; the final part contains many of the resources the school developed, including summaries of over 100 children's books and suggestions for their use.

This book shows how popular and easily obtainable children's stories can be used to help them understand and manage their emotions. The books are listed, there are summaries of the stories, and there are lots of suggestions and ideas for using them.

Acknowledgement

Some of the material and approaches described in this book were developed by Leeds Healthy Schools and are based on work done by schools in the Leeds Education Action Zone – Bankside Primary School, Ebor Gardens Primary School, Hillcrest Primary School, Hillcrest Primary School, Leopold Primary School, Primrose High School and Shakespeare Primary School.

Contents

Rainbow Fish

Emotional Illiteracy

My name is Jane Fisher. I'm a teacher in a primary school.

When I was seven years old my father died. My memories of him are all of a very poorly man. He was quiet and gentle, and would spend many hours with me reading books as he lay in bed or on the sofa. Sometimes we would go out and walk, slowly, holding each other's hands, but towards the end he could only walk to the end of the road. Before he died he bought me the book 'Jonathan Livingston Seagull'. Perhaps he already knew the importance of emotional literacy.

When he died in hospital, for the next two weeks my mother continued to leave the house to go 'visit him in hospital'. How long this pretence would have gone on I don't know, but one tea-time my grandmother let it slip that he had died. I remember the tears flowing down my face. So many tears that the cream crackers I was clenching in my hands became soggy and crumbled on to the table. (I still can't eat cream crackers, the memory of that vision stays with me!) My mother never took my brother or me to my father's funeral. It was her belief that it was best for us not to go.

Following the trauma of my father's death I began to suffer from poor eye sight. I was taken from specialist to specialist. On one occasion I would be severely short sighted, on another long sighted. What had happened was that the muscles in my eyes had stopped functioning properly, and I couldn't focus. Now I can see this as an extremely powerful example of the power of a child's emotional state to affect their physical wellbeing. My brain was so fully occupied coping with the loss of my father that sight did not seem to matter, and certainly the messages weren't getting from my brain to my eye muscles. Nearly two years later as my mother cleaned the kitchen and put down newspapers on the wet floor, I walked in and bent over to read one of them. To her joy I could once again see small print.

If my emotions could cause such a clear physical reaction, how many other children are severely hampered by the emotions they feel?

Following the death of my father, a group of boys at school told me that my father was not dead but had gone off with another woman. I had never seen my father really ill in hospital, I had not been to his grave, and how I wished he was still alive, even if he was not living with me.

I went home and told my mother what I thought was good news. Imagine the scene as I rushed into the house to tell my mother that "Dad's not dead, he's just with another woman, a boy at school told me so!" "Don't be so ridiculous, "said my mother as she burst into floods of tears. I soon learnt not to mention what I was sure was a fact, that my father was still alive, just not with us. The boys at school continued to tell me stories. They had seen him on the golf course; they had seen him in WH Smiths - always, of course, with the other woman. How many times I went out on my bike, cycling round the golf course in search of him. I caught the bus into town, in search of him. A confused child, not knowing what to believe and not talking to anyone. If I told my mum I made her cry, and if I told the teachers perhaps they would tell me that he really was dead.

My mother continued to grieve. At night I would lie in my bed hearing her crying. Sometimes I would get out of bed and go to try and comfort her, but I could never stop her crying. I thought that maybe if I worked really hard at school and was really good, that might make her happy again. So I worked and worked, but it didn't seem to make any difference. It didn't matter if I came second in my test, still I would hear her crying. As a child I began to believe that only being the very very best might make her happy. And how I tried. But I could never come top, and I could never stop those tears. A child desperately trying to please but failing, never understanding that even if I had come top, my mother would have still been crying at night. So I continued to strive.

I was not alone. My brother, too, had lost his father. Same family, same father, but a different outcome. While I was busy trying to be Little Miss Perfect, my brother quickly learnt that that didn't work. His response was to try a different tack and become Mr Naughty. "This will get me noticed!" We would go shopping and mother, with her bags in one hand, would always have to hold on to him with the other because he might run off. But she knew I would be good, so I could walk behind. So his tactic seemed to work - at least if you were naughty you got noticed.

Because I tried so hard I did well at school. Not top, maybe, but pretty good. The teachers liked me, I achieved, and started on the route to a successful career. My brother was different. His attitude seemed to be 'if I can't be good enough, then I'll just not bother trying!' Within a year he had become so troublesome at school that the headteacher told my mother they really couldn't cope with him any more. He was sent away to boarding school.

Two children. One family. The same events. But different responses and different consequences, affecting the entire lives of those involved. What happened to us – to me, my brother, and to our poor mother who seemed at a total loss to understand what was happening to her or her family, or why – can be attributed to our inability to recognise, verbalise and process our emotions. Because we were not equipped to handle our emotions we were at their mercy. Like cancers, uncontrolled, they grew until they dominated our existences and shaped our futures.

I don't think what happened to my family was unusual. A little more extreme, perhaps, but not untypical. Thankfully many more teachers and parents are now aware of the ways in which a child's emotions can affect his or her growth and development. Daniel Goleman's 'Emotional Intelligence' has become a best seller, and the title has passed into the language of pedagogy. I find the term 'intelligence' not the most helpful to apply to the emotions. It suggests something that you either have or don't have, something you are born with. Evidence and experience tell me that the ability to touch, recognise, talk about, process, respond to and control the emotions can be taught, and that this is an important component of education. So I prefer the term 'emotional literacy'.

This book gives an account of an approach taken at Hovingham Primary School to supporting children's emotional growth through books. It identifies a wide range of popular stories and shows how they can be used to help children prepare for and deal with the experiences and feelings of daily life. It describes how we initiated and developed this work, and the rationale on which it is based.

Why Emotional Literacy?

So what is emotional literacy? Why is it important? And how can reading stories to children help them to talk about and understand their feelings?

To begin with, let's get some perspective on the world we inhabit, and then let's relate this to the United Kingdom. In his wonderful and thought-provoking book 'If the World Were a Village', David J Smith suggests that we can appreciate the range and variety of the gobal population by imagining it as a village of 100 people.

In this village

- 64 would be Asians and 12 Europeans. Five would be from North America and 13 would be Africans. 21 people would be Chinese and 22 would speak a Chinese dialect. Only nine would speak English.

- 20 of the villagers would be under 10 years old, and 40 would be under 20. Only 10 would be over 60.

- 32 would be Christians and 19 Muslims. 15 would subscribe to no religious denomination at all.

- Only 30 of the village's inhabitants would always have enough to eat. 50 would not eat regularly and would be hungry some of the time, and another 20 would be starving slowly to death.

- 17 would be unable to read.

- The richest 20 people would own almost half of the community's entire wealth. 20 would earn less than 60p a day.

The United Kingdom is racially and culturally diverse, and Smith's analogy will have a resonance for many people living here. It's possible to take his idea and extend it a little further. For example

- The village would have 89 people who were heterosexual and 11 who were homosexual.

'If the World Were a Village', David J Smith, A&C Black

- 80 would live in sub-standard housing.

- 17 would be unable to read or write.

- Almost half would suffer from malnutrition.

- 1 villager would be near death and 1 would be newly born. 39 would be under 19 years old.

- 1 would have a college education.

- 1 would own a computer.

If you woke up this morning healthy, you are in a better state than one million people in the world who will not survive the week. If you have money in your wallet or purse, perhaps some change in a dish somewhere, you are among the top 8% of the worlds wealthy. If your parents are alive and still married you are rare.

In multi-cultural Britain the social, racial and economic implications of this world perspective are bound to impinge on the lives of many families and children. So let us take note of some of the things that are happening in our own country. These figures are based on information from the NSPCC and other charitable organisations, the National Statistical Office, and gathered from several media sources, including The Guardian and the BBC.

- Although the rate of teenage suicide fell between 1992 and 2002, there are still 20,000 suicide attempts made each year by adolescents. (one every 26 minutes). The charity Depression Alliance estimates that each year more than 2 million children attend GP's surgeries with some kind of psychological or emotional problem.

- Britain has one of the highest suicide rates in Europe. The Samaritans estimate that in the general population there is one suicide attempt every 82 minutes. Childline reports (15 March 2006) that 'worrying numbers of the UK's young people are considering taking their own lives in a desperate attempt to escape their problems', and reveals an alarming 14% rise in calls to its helpline from suicidal children.

- Each year 44,000 young people reach hospital having injured or poisoned themselves. The suicide rate for 18-24-year-old males has jumped from 58 deaths per million of population in 1974 to 170 deaths per million in 1997. In October 1999, the government reported that the number of young males who commit suicide each year in the UK had doubled over the last ten years.

- A UK Mental Health Foundation survey published in February 2001 revealed that half of university students showed signs of clinical anxiety whilst more than 10% suffered from clinical depression.

- Suicide is the second most common cause of death for young men, second only to road accidents.

- 1 in 4 people know of someone who has committed suicide.

- Britain's teenage pregnancy rate is the highest in Europe. In 2002 there were 39,286 teen pregnancies recorded. The government has spent more than £60 million to tackle the problem but has so far failed to halt the rise. In 2003 almost six and a half thousand girls under 16 became pregnant. Over half of these had abortions.

- 200,000 children under 16 have lost a parent by death.

- 68% of pupils say they are bullied at some stage in their school lives.

- Although the number of children on child protection registers is falling, in March 2005 there were still almost 26,000 children listed.

- 1 in every 4 children under 16 will experience parents divorcing. About a quarter of all parents are single parents.

- At any time 1 in 6 adults suffer from a neurotic disorder.

- In England and Wales at least one child is killed every week, the majority by their parents or carers. There are over 100 case reviews each year involving the death or serious injury of a child as a result of neglect or abuse.

Given this perspective on the world and on our own country, the need children have for help in dealing with emotions – their own and other people's – is clear. Our emotions and the way we handle them affects our relationships and can have important consequences for our physical and mental well-being.

There is plenty of evidence that emotions can be at the root of disease, and may even make the difference between life and death. Consider these findings from surveys in the USA:

- Among several hundred medical students at the University of North Carolina who were rated for hostility levels while in their early twenties, those with chronic anger were seven times more likely than their peers to be dead by their mid forties.

- Of 100 patients preparing to go through Bone marrow transplants at the University of Minnesota (an extremely high-risk procedure) 12 of the 13 most depressed were dead with in a year. But of the 87 who were not depressed, 34 were still alive at the end of a year.

- In a Harvard study, 122 men who had their first heart attack were evaluated for optimism. Eight years later, of the 25 most pessimistic men, 21 had died. Of the 25 most optimistic men, just 6 had died.

These three studies linking emotional states and disease are supported by more than a hundred others. The University of California combined them into a meta-analysis showing that such afflictive emotions double a person's susceptibility to disease of every kind. On the positive side, the intelligent management of difficult emotions seems to help the body fight disease. **Given the growing evidence of the link between emotions and health, it seems obvious that an educational program in emotional literacy is valuable preventive mind/body medicine and should be an essential for schools.**

Our emotions affect our overall wellbeing, and not surprisingly this includes our ability to learn. How and why does this happen?

Emotions and the Brain

The following is a much simplified explanation of how the brain works. The relationships between the various elements have only recently been understood, and the exact nature of their linkages and effects is still being studied. However, we can think of the brain as having four main areas: the limbic system, the amygdola, the cerebellum and the cerebral cortex.

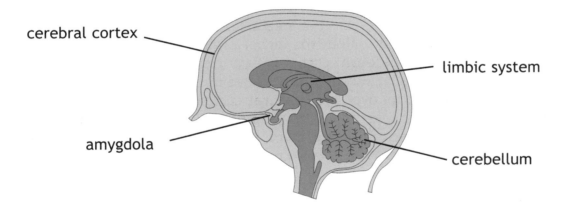

The amygdola (the term comes from the Greek word for almond, and is so called because it is about the size and shape of an almond) sits on top of the spinal chord. The cerebellum is located at the base of the brain. This is the area of the brain which deals with the most primitive animal functions, and the amygdola and cerebellum are sometimes referred to together as the 'reptilian brain'. The reptilian brain is usually off-duty and passive, but at times of stress it takes priority over all the other brain areas, responding to stress with a 'fight', 'flight', 'freeze' or 'flock' reflex. These are the most basic survivial strategies, which have evolved to protect the organism and the species. Long ago they would have helped our ancestors preserve themselves in the face of danger, and they still come into play when we are threatened or attacked. But in the complexities of modern living stress often takes different forms and so these basic brain functions show their effects in other ways.

A stressed child who is exhibiting a 'flight' response will not want to come to school; he or she will try to avoid every opportunity to learn. A child showing a 'fight' response to stress will be aggressive and will probably exhibit behavioural problems. A child who has frozen will appear to be disengaged, 'switched off'. They will be uninterested and will be motivated to fail to achieve rather than to succeed. A child exhibiting a 'flock' response will seek reassurance and safety with others. This is the child who seems unable to do anything on their own, who always needs someone with them and always turns to a peer or adult for support.

The limbic system (sometimes called the mid-brain) is the area which deals with emotions and feelings. Love, hate, jealousy, anger, anxiety, joy, sorrow are all associated with increased activity in this section of the brain. The limbic system also seems able to 'store' emotions connected with particular experiences. The obvious relevance to education is that if a negative emotion is repeatedly associated with a learning experience, then all learning will provoke an unfavourable reaction, and will be subconsciously rejected. We will avoid it.

The cerebral cortex is the outer layer of the brain, a sort of coating a few millimeters thick, which wraps over the whole of the brain. It manages the senses, particularly sight and hearing, processes information, deals with logic and reasoning. This part of the brain is not fully developed until a child is at least seven and sometimes as old as nine. It is the area associated with academic learning, and because of this is sometimes called 'the higher brain', or 'the thinking brain'. The important feature of the cerebral cortex is that it can only function properly if the reptilian and limbic brains allow it to. At times of high emotion or stress either or both will seize priority over the cerebral cortex and reduce its capacity and efficiency. At its simplest level this simply confirms what every teacher knows: a child who is safe, secure, happy, calm, in a positive frame of mind and who feels good will learn better than one who isn't.

So the reptilian brain responds to stress, the limbic system processes emotions and the cerebral cortex handles the information reaching the brain through the senses. Given this, it is not surprising that research into the way the brain learns concludes that emotional health is fundamental to effective learning. The reptilian brain must be switched off and the limbic system calm in order to allow the cerebral cortex to perform its higher functions. A secure, stable and caring home environment is a major requirement for the individual to achieve this state. Sensitive teaching based on an understanding of how children learn is essential.

It is also necessary for the student to be able to manage and control his or her own emotions - to be emotionally literate - and to be aware of the way their brain acquires and processes information. Basically, a student who learns to learn is much more likely to succeed. According to a report from the National Center for Clinical Infant Programs, the most critical element for a student's success in school is an understanding of how to learn (Goleman, Emotional Intelligence, p.193). The key ingredients of this understanding are:

- Confidence
- Curiosity

- Intentionality
- Self-control
- Relatedness
- Capacity to communicate
- Ability to cooperate

These traits are all aspects of Emotional Intelligence. Emotional Intelligence has proven a better predictor of future success than traditional methods like the GPA, IQ, and standardised test scores. Hence, the great interest in Emotional Intelligence on the part of corporations, universities, and schools nationwide. The idea of Emotional Intelligence has inspired research and curriculum development throughout these facilities. Researchers have concluded that people who manage their own feelings well and deal effectively with others are more likely to live contented lives. Furthermore, happy people are more apt to retain information and do so more effectively than dissatisfied people.

Building one's Emotional Intelligence has a lifelong impact. Many parents and educators, alarmed by increasing levels of conflict in young schoolchildren – from low self-esteem to early drug and alcohol use to depression – are rushing to teach students the skills they need to help them develop their Emotional Intelligence. And in corporations, the inclusion of Emotional Intelligence in training programs has helped employees cooperate better and has improved motivation, thereby increasing productivity and profits.

'Emotional Intelligence is a master aptitude, a capacity that profoundly affects all other abilities, either facilitating or interfering with them' (Goleman, Emotional Intelligence, p.80).

Developing Emotional Literacy

Unfortunately, we cannot expect children always to present themselves in school with their reptilian and limbic brains relaxed and passive! The stresses and strains of modern living – let alone the school playground – often militate against this, and there are far too many things in a child's life over which we have no control to assume that we can rely on there being a suitable climate for learning. However, we can and we should equip children to manage their emotions, and a key part of this is being able to express them in a controlled and effective manner. To be able to do this is to be emotionally literate.

Throughout history, human beings have had the problem of communicating feelings through language. Emotional literacy is really about understanding the colours and moods of our emotions, and learning to use them to create harmonious relationships with others. It is essential for children to learn these skills early, in school and at home. We should invest time and resources to show children how emotions are an integral part of human nature, and that they need not grow up to use the negative, self defeating ways of relating. We need to empower children by making them understand that their emotions can be controlled. They can switch on emotions such as fear and doubt, which affect thoughts and actions deeply, and they can switch on positive feelings of hope and well-being, knowing that these feelings are better for our bodies and our relationships. They have a choice, and by becoming emotionally literate they can learn to control their emotions rather than being their prisoner. Daniel Goleman argues that Emotional Intelligence is of much greater importance than 'academic' intelligence in developing a well-rounded person. He continues 'at best IQ contributes about 20 per cent to the factors that determine life success, which leaves 80 per cent to other forces.'

Positive and negative thoughts can cause major changes in the way the brain processes, stores and retrieves information. Just as different foods will have an effect on the body's neurotransmitters, so too will one's mental state. If a person, adult or child, is experiencing intense, positive emotions (on an emotional 'high') their brain will release endorphins, which in turn will trigger the flow of acetylcholine, the vital neuro-transmitter that orders new memories to be imprinted in various parts of the brain. Ronald Kotulak describes acetylcholine as 'the oil that makes the memory machine function. When it dries up, the machine freezes.' Not only is acetylcholine essential for imprinting new memories, it is also needed for retrieving old ones.

In emotionally literate organisations, people receive praise and thanks and feel valued, have high self esteem, are able to give and receive praise, nurture each other and lead a full and rich life beyond the organisation. In a school context, learners need a strong sense of self and an empathic awareness of others, awareness of the role and power of emotions in learning and decision making, a sound basis for their values and morality, a tolerance of diversity and difference and a sense of meaning and purpose in their lives. Emotional literacy needs to be fostered directly though employing a range of knowledge, skills, experiences and feelings. This should encompass the following development areas:

- Conscious awareness, particularly in extending the vocabulary of feelings.

- Understanding thoughts, feelings and actions as they relate to learning and achievement, decision making and relationships.

- Managing feelings so that we can be more effective in meeting our needs without violating the interests of others.

- Promoting self esteem so that people feel good about themselves and about each other.

- Managing conflict to achieve win-win outcomes through effective anger management and better interpersonal skills.

- Understanding groups to contribute more effectively in group settings.

- Communication skills to promote appropriate expression of feelings and thoughts.

Goleman elaborated an Emotional Competence framework that encompasses:

- Self-awareness – knowing one's internal states, preferences, resources and intuitions
- Emotional awareness
- Accurate self assessment
- Self-confidence
- Self-regulation – managing one's internal states, impulses and resources
- Self-control
- Trustworthiness
- Conscientiousness
- Adaptability
- Innovation
- Motivation – emotional tendencies that guide or facilitate reaching goals
- Achievement drive
- Commitment
- Initiative
- Optimism, persistence and resilience.

There are close links between Goleman's emotional competences and the skills needed for successful social relationships. Social competence has at its core understanding other people, which relies on empathy and the awareness of others' feelings, needs and concerns. By focusing on these things we aim to help children to develop their skills of communication and self management, and to help them work with others and resolve conflict situations.

There are, of course, huge implications for the management and staff of a school. If children are to be emotionally literate, so must the staff be! This has been recognised by Southampton LEA, so far – to the best of the writer's knowledge – the only local authority to have adopted the development of emotional literacy as a strategic objective. Southampton's guidance says

'Developing the Emotional Literacy of staff in school is central to developing the Emotional Literacy of the children, and some of the key characteristics of the most Emotionally Literate staff include:
- Being infectiously optimistic
- Being a good listener
- Showing commitment
- Being a celebrator of others successes

- Having high self regard
- Being emotionally resilient
- Having a high stress tolerance'

Southampton's guidelines suggest that the emotional climate and school culture will be determined to a great extent by how many of the staff possess the characteristics listed above, and how few of the staff are depressed or leaking cynicism!

Developing Emotional Literacy in School

A programme for developing emotional literacy in school needs to be introduced with some care. There have been occasions in the teaching profession over the last two decades when morale has not been high. Simply telling colleagues that they must be cheerful and positive runs the risk of eliciting a dusty response. However, positive leadership, a deliberate focus in staff meetings and day-to-day interactions on successes and achievements, and an appreciation by all of the pleasures and rewards to be found in the company of children can do much to enrich even the most jaundiced

An important part of our work at Hovingham was the establishment of a set of statements designed to promote effort, achievement and positive behaviour. These were developed as part of the Leeds Healthy School Programme. Some of the positive affirmations are listed.

I can suggest one way we can make our school more friendly.

I try to follow our school and classroom rules.

I know how/who to ask for help

I can say one thing I would like to get better at.

I can tell you how I look after myself.

I think before I make changes that affect my health.

I can say how I feel.

I try to take care of the world around me.

I can share.

I know what respect means.

I try to tell the truth even when it is hard.

I try to keep going when things are difficult.

I listen to what you say: I show that I am listening to you.

I try to use words that make the world a better place (like please, sorry and thank you).

I can set a target for myself.

I suggest one way we can make our school a healthy school.

I try to be considerate of other peoples needs.

I realise what I do affects how others feel.

I try to be patient with people.

I know what trust means.

I cooperate with others in work and in play.

I know how to help others when they are in trouble.

I can take care of the plants and animals in our world.

I can say how I can improve the world around me.

I notice that we are the same, I notice that we are different. To be both is ok.

I treat all adults and children with respect.

I can listen well to good things about me.

I value my achievements. I am proud of what I can do.

I can learn from my mistakes.

I can tell you how I look after myself.

I know what to do if I see anyone being hurt.

I treat people how I would like to be treated.

My past has been good. I can make my future even better.

These statements pervade the life of the school and are addressed through many activities. One of the most significant is the development of guidance and resources to enable staff to use books and stories to promote the statements and to reinforce them.

The first step in our approach to developing emotional literacy through books and stories was to build up our book stock so that we had a range of resources suitable for addressing various aspects of emtional development. A search was made on the Internet to find suggestions which we could use to help select the books. A list from the Southampton Library services and the website www.nelig.com (national emotional literacy interest group) were the most useful, but in the end it seemed that the best way to choose the books was simply to sit down and read through a host of children's books, collecting all the ones to which I felt our children would respond. I tried to select books short enough to use in story time sessions, as stories for assemblies and in circle time or nurture groups. Most of the books are extensively illustrated and contain beautiful and often evocative pictures. I felt this was important, especially for younger children. The objective of the selection was to provide a collection of stories that would provoke discussion. The obvious advantage of using stories is that, by featuring characters which are fictitious and with whom children can identify, events and situations close to the children's own experiences can be presented and discussed in a non-threatening way.

The books were sorted into categories which related to the main feelings or topics within each story. This sorting offers teachers a guide to the books which may be most useful to read in certain circumstances. However, this is only a start. Often other topics arise as the children begin to talk.

In 2004 the school was able to raise more money and the library was extended to include 114 different titles. We held a whole school staff meeting each time a new selection of books was purchased to give all the staff the chance to see the new additions. Every book has a label inside the cover which gives a brief outline of the contents of the book and indicates the emotions and feelings that are the focus of the book. All staff were also given a list of the books and descriptive information about their themes and contents.

The way the books are used varies from one teacher to another. The usual approach is for a book to be read to a small group of children by a teaching assistant or learning mentor. Books are also often read aloud during story sessions, when the class is able to talk about their responses to the issues raised. The stories encourage the children to share their feelings and discuss the emotions explored.

Using stories to encourage children to talk enables them to detach themselves from their own feelings and explore them within the safety of a character or persona. Sometimes a puppet or doll is used as an adjunct to the reading, which extends the 'safety zone' by enabling children to talk about their own feelings at a distance.

Each week one of the books is used in assembly. Sometimes children are involved in acting out the story for those watching. The moral values which underpin the story are emphasised and the children are encouraged to think about how their own behaviour affects the feelings of others. Some of the books have very little text, and these stimulate the children to use their language to describe the situations that the pictures portray. Picture books can also be used with older children as starters for them to create their own texts, spoken or written, describing what they see in the pictures.

Many of the books can be used across the curriculum, where there are opportunities to explore the story using a range of visual, auditory, and kinaesthetic learning styles. In Year 2 recently the children looked at the story 'The Rainbow Fish'. We explored the story in literacy, working first on the setting and characters. In Art we made pictures of the setting using wax crayon and watercolour wash, or pastels. Later, when we had discussed the stories again, the children added the characters with collage materials to their picture of the setting. They decided if their picture was to show the beginning of the story when the Rainbow Fish has all the shiny scales, or whether it was later in the story when some of the other fish would have shiny scales too. Later the children made fish using tissue scales which they glued onto bubble wrap. When all the characters had been made the children were able to role play the story, acting out the story in class and in assembly. In other lessons during the week the children created pictures of the fish on the computer and made clay models. Many of the activities were planned so that the children had to work co-operatively with each other. For example, they created the pictures with partners, took it in turns to play at being the Rainbow Fish, and worked together to make the characters. By the end of the week the children were able to recount the story, and more importantly talk about the importance of sharing. The work that the children produced was put on show in the hall, and other classes were encouraged to look at the display and read the story again.

On the pages which follow is a list of the books in our collection and the particular emotions to which they relate. After this there are summaries of the books, together with some tips for using them. The Resources section contains examples of some of the bookplates from Hovingham (all of them are on the CD which goes with this book). Finally, we have included examples of 'I Can Statements', Word Frames for you to use in creating your own bookplates and some sample games. These are also on the CD.

Emotional Literacy Booklist

The following pages contain the booklist we compiled to be the core of our resources for developing emotional literacy. The list appears here in alphabetical order of title. It is included on the CD which accompanies this books as a Microsoft Excel spreadsheet, which will allow users to sort it by author or publisher, or by the emotions addressed, and to add their own comments. Our notes on the titles and our guidance on how the books may be used follow this list. We have not included ISBNs, but most bookshops and any library should be able to obtain further information about any of the titles. As far as we know, all are in print at the time of writing this book.

The list allocates up to three categories to each book. We arrived at these by analysing the stories and for each one listing the emotions or feelings which featured most prominently in the story. We reduced these to no more than three for each, which we felt could form the basis of an assembly or the introduction to a discussion session.

Strictly speaking some of the terms on our list are not actually emotions, but they are connected with feelings likely to be experienced by children. Some of them are qualities which we think it is important for children to consider and talk about. Some of the distinctions are also a little arbitrary: for example, what is the difference between bravery and courage? We suggest you read the stories and we hope you will see why we have chosen one term rather than another. You may also want to change our suggested focus. It is possible to use most of these stories in a variety of ways; our approach is only one of many.

Title	Author	Publisher	Cat 1	Cat 2	Cat 3
A Cat and a Dog	Masurel. C. & Kolar, B.	North-South Books (2001)	Friendship	Unkindness	Kindness
A Cultivated Wolf	Bloom, B.	Siphano Books (1999)	Aggression	Friendship	Persistence
A Friend for Little Bear	Horse, H.	Walker Books (2003)	Greed	Friendship	
A Special Something	Fearnley, J.	Egmont Books (2000)	Jealousy	Love	
All Kinds of Bodies	Brownjohn, E.	Tango Books (2002)	Respect	Understanding	
All Kinds of Feelings	Brownjohn, E.	Tango Books (1995)	Happiness	Sadness	Differences
All Kinds of People	Damon, E.	Tango Books (1995)	Empathy	Differences	Understanding
Baby on Board	Gray, K. & Nayler, S.	Hodder (2004)	Jealousy	Family life	Babies
Badgers Bad Mood	Varley, S.	Scholastic (2002)	Appreciation	Sadness	
Badgers Parting Gifts	Varley, S.	Picture Lions (1994)	Bereavement	Sadness	
Big Bird and Little Bird	Widdowson, Kay	Tango Books (2001)	Perseverance	Enjoyment	
Big Book of Families	Anholt, C. & Anholt, L.	Walker Books (2000)	Love	Differences	Understanding
Billy & the Big New School	Anholt, C. & Anholt, L.	Orchard Books (2004)	Anxiety	Friendship	
Billywise	Nicholls, J. & Cockcroft, J.	Bloomsbury (2004)	Being afraid	Perseverance	Bravery
Bored Claude	Newton, J.	Bloomsbury (2003)	Boredom	Co-operation	
Cleversticks	Brazell, D.	Picture Lions (2002)	Confidence	Persistence	
Crocodiles Masterpiece	Velthuijs, M.	Andersen Press (2001)	Appreciation		
David Gets in Trouble	Shannon, D.	Scholastic (2002)	Naughtiness	Apologising	Forgiving
David Goes to School	Shannon, D.	Scholastic (1999)	Naughtiness	Forgiving	
Don't Let Go	Willis, J. & Ross, D.	Andersen Press (2004)	Perseverance	Love	
Don't Be Horrid, Henry	Simon, F.	Orion Childrens (200)	Unkindness	Jealousy	Siblings
Dr. Dog	Cole, Babette	Red Fox (1996)	Health		
Excuse Me!	Kopelke, L.	Pocket Books (2004)	Manners		
Five Little Friends	Dyer, S.	Bloomsbury (2001)	Greed	Sharing	Friendship
Fran's Friend	Bruce, L. & Beardshaw, R.	Bloomsbury (2004)	Friendship		
Frog	Browne, J.	Red Fox (2003)	Being afraid	Courage	Caring
Frog and the Stranger	Velthuijs, M.	Andersen (1995)	Individuality	Kindness	Friendship
Frog and the Treasure	Velthuijs, M.	Andersen (2004)	Friendship	Bravery	
Frog finds a Friend	Velthuijs, M.	Andersen (2004)	Friendship	Caring	
Frog is Hero	Velthuijs, M.	Andersen (1997)	Pride	Courage	
Giraffes Can't Dance	Andreae, G. & Parker-Rees, G.	Orchard Books (2001)	Differences	Persistence	
Good Baby, Bad Baby	Newman, N.	Picture Lions (2003)	Differences	Moodiness	
Good Days Bad Days	Anholt, C. & Anholt, L.	Orchard Books (2004	Family life	Happiness	Sadness
Goodbye Mousie	Harris, R.	Simon & Schuster (2003)	Bereavement	Sadness	
Green Poems	Bennett, J. (Ed)	OUP (1999)	Environment	Caring	

Title	Author	Publisher	Cat 1	Cat 2	Cat 3
Guess How Much I Love You	McBratney, S.	Walker Books (1996)	Love	Caring	Individuality
Hair in Funny Places	Cole, Babette	Red Fox (2001)	Growing up	Relationships	
Have You Seen Elvis?	Murray, A.	Macmillan (2002)	Aggression	Friendship	
Home Before Dark	Beck, I.	Scholastic Hippo (2003)	Being afraid	Courage	Perseverance
Hoot and Holler	Brown A.	Red Fox (2002)	Shyness	Love	Appreciation
I Don't Care	Moses, B.	Hodder Wayland (1998)	Caring	Kindness	Appreciation
I Feel Happy	Murphy, M.	DK Ink (2000)	General		
I Love You, Blue Kangaroo	Clark, E.	Andersen Press (2005)	Love		
I Will Not Ever Never Eat a Tomato	Child, L.	Candlewick Press (2003)	Health		
I'll Always Love You	Lewis, P.	Little Tiger Press (2001)	Love	Forgiving	
I'm Lonely	Moses, B.	Hodder Wayland (1997)	Loneliness		
I'm Not Invited	Bluthenthal, D.	Atheneum Books (2003)	Loneliness	Sadness	
I'm Not Your Friend	McBratney, S.	Picture Lions (2002)	Friendship	Forgiving	Being afraid
I'm Sorry	McBratney, S.	Picture Lions (2001)	Friendship	Sadness	Apologising
I'm Special	Green, J.	Hodder Wayland (1999)	Understanding	Consideration	Caring
Is That What Friends Do?	Newman, M.	Hutchinson (1998)	Friendship	Loneliness	Apologising
It Was You, Blue Kangaroo	Clark, E.	Doubleday (2002)	Honesty	Unkindness	
I've Got Nits	Brownlow, M.	Ragged Bears (2001)	Health		
Jennifer Jones Wont Leave Me Alone	Wishinsky, F.	Corgi Children's (2004)	Love	Loneliness	
Jonathan Livingston Seagull	Bache, R.	Harper Collins (19994)	Perseverance	Individuality	
Just Like You	Fearnley, J.	Egmont Books (2004)	Love	Caring	
Kitty Princess & the Newspaper Dress	Dickinson, T.	Orchard Books (2004))	Manners	Apologising	
L is for Loving	Wilson-Max, K.	Hyperion Books (1999)	General		
Letters from Around the World	Maclaren, Thando	Tango Books (2004)	Empathy	Differences	Understanding
Lilly's Purple Plastic Purse	Henkes, K.	Hodder (1998)	Naughtiness	Apologising	Forgiving
Little Beaver and the Echo	Macdonald, A.	Walker Books (2002)	Friendship	Loneliness	
Little Snail's Big Surprise	Dijs, C.	Childs Play (1999)	Siblings		
Lost: One Green Dog	Biet, P.	Siphano (2000)	Confidence	Individuality	
Martha's Friends	Damon, E.	Tango Books (1998)	Bullying	Shyness	Friendship
Mine	Oram, H.	Frances Lincoln (1992)	Sharing	Selfishness	
Mole and the Baby Bird	Newman, M.	Bloomsbury (2003)	Love	Consideration	
Mouse, Mole and the Falling Star	Benjamin, A.	Little Tiger (2002)	Friendship	Greed	
My Friend Bear	Alborough, J.	Walker Books (2004)	Friendship	Loneliness	
My Nose, Your Nose	Walsh, M.	Corgi (2003)	Differences	Similarities	Empathy
No David!	Shannon, D.	Scholastic (2003)	Naughtiness	Forgiving	Love

Title	Author	Publisher	Cat 1	Cat 2	Cat 3
No Matter What	Glori, D.	Bloomsbury (2003)	Love	Bereavement	Caring
One World	Foreman, M.	Andersen (2004)	Environment	Caring	
Petar's Song	Mitchell, P. & Birch, C.	Frances Lincoln (2004)	War	Pain	Hope
Princess Snooty Cat	Damon, E.	Tango Books (2002)	Kindness	Loneliness	Rudeness
Rainbow Fish & the Big Blue Whale	Pfister, M.	North-South (2002)	Courage	Being afraid	
Rainbow Fish to the Rescue	Pfister, M.	North-South (1998)	Courage	Friendship	Forgiving
Rapunzel	Roberts, L.	Chrysalis (2004)	Love	Friendship	
Really Brave Tim	Prater, J.	Red Fox (2001)	Courage		
Rude Mule	Nascimbeni, B.	Macmillan (2002)	Rudeness	Unkindness	
Sitting Ducks	Bedard, B.	Walker Books (2002)	Friendship		
So Hungry	Morden, D. & Carpenter, S.	Pont Books (2004)	Hunger	Sharing	
Sophie and the New Baby	Anholt, C. & Anholt, L.	Orchard Books (2004)	New siblings	Change	
Tadpole's Promise	Willis, J. & Ross, T.	Atheneum Books (2005)	Love	Honesty	
The Colour of Home	Hoffman, M. & Littlewood, K.	Frances Lincoln (2003)	Differences		
The Gossipy Parrot	Roddie, S.	Bloomsbury (2004)	Gossiping	Rudeness	
The Happy Hedgehog	Pfister, M.	North-South Books (2003)	Enjoyment	Individuality	
The Lion Who Wanted to Love	Andreae, G. & Wojtowycz, D.	Orchard Books (2004)	Love	Bravery	Persistence
The Polar Bear & the Snow Cloud	Cabrera, Jane	Macmillan (2004)	Loneliness	Friendship	
The Rainbow Fish	Pfister, M.	North-South Books (2000)	Greed	Sharing	Friendship
The Red Tree	Tan, S.	Lothian Books (2003)	Loneliness	Sadness	Hope
The Richest Crocodile in the World	Postgate, D.	Picture Lions (2004)	Friendship	Sharing	Love
The Selfish Crocodile	Charles, F.	Bloomsbury (1999)	Selfishness	Courage	Sharing
The Smartest Giant in Town	Donaldson, J.	Macmillan (2002)	Sharing	Kindness	Appreciation
The Three Grumpies	Wight, T.	Bloomsbury (2005)	Moodiness		
The Very Lazy Ladybird	Finn, I.	Little Tiger Press (2003)	Laziness		
The World Came to My Place Today	Readman, J. & Roberts, L.H.	Eden Books (2004)	Environment		
Three Cheers for Ostrich	Simon, F.	Gullane (2001)	Caring	Kindness	
Tissue Please!	Kopelke, L.	Simon & Schuster (2004)	Manners		
TrueLove	Cole, Babette	Red Fox (2002)	Jealousy	Love	Forgiveness
Up in Heaven	Clark, E.C.	Andersen Press (2004)	Grief	Sadness	
Voices in the Park	Browne, A.	Corgi (1999)	Friendship	Kindness	Consideration
Wanda's First Day at School	Sperring, M.	Chicken House (2005)	Differences	Starting school	
What Colour is Love?	Strachan, L. & Wojtowycz, D.	Bloomsbury (2004)	Love		
What is Peace?	Damon, E.	Tango Books (2004)	Peace	Friendship	Sharing
Whatever Wanda Wanted	Wisdom, J.	Dial Books (2002)	Greed	Rudeness	

Title	Author	Publisher	Cat 1	Cat 2	Cat 3
Where Are You, Blue Kangaroo?	Clark, E.	Doubleday (2001)	Friendship	Caring	
Who Loves You, Little Beetle?	Dijs, C.	Childs Play (1997)	Love	Individuality	
Willy and Hugh	Browne, A.	Red Fox (2000)	Friendship	Courage	Bullying
Willy the Wizard	Browne, A.	Corgi (2003)	Courage	Perseverance	Bullying
With Love	Cooling, W. (Ed)	Orchard Books (2004)	Enjoyment		
Wonder Goal	Foreman, M.	Red Fox (2004)	Hope	Ambition	
You Choose	Sharratt, N. & Goodhart, P.	Picture Corgi (2004)	Choice	Ambition	
You've Got Dragons	Cave, K.	Hodder (2002)	Worry	Being afraid	Courage
Zed the Zebra	Vrombaut, A.	Hodder (2001)	Boasting		

Notes on the Books

The following pages describe the books on our emotional literacy booklist. We provide a short summary/introductions, plus a few indicators of the ways they can be used and what you might expect to arise from them.

We recommend that you should always read the story yourself first before using it with children, but because of the sensitive nature of the subject matter children may need special preparation for some of the stories. In such cases we've said so in the text and indicated it with a ●✦ symbol in the margin.

A Cat and a Dog
by Claire Masurel, Bob Kolar

A cat and a dog live in the house, but they are not friends, in fact they are sworn enemies, until they discover that they need each other and become the best of friends. Very simple text and pictures make this a great book for younger children. This is a classic story of dog and cat, but it is also about brothers and sisters, or children in the class. They fight, they say nasty things to each other, they won't share, they don't play together, and then one day they discover that they can do things to help each other and that life can be much more fun if they become friends. Lots to talk about and discuss, and a simple message and lesson for us all to learn.

A Cultivated Wolf
by Pascal Biet

A hungry wolf descends on a farm full of educated animals. The only way for the wolf to be admitted to the farm is to complete a series of challenges, and the wolf is soon going from school to library to village bookstore. A Cultivated Wolf tells a story that proves that anyone can change their ways and that there is more to life than eating grandmothers! It is a book about dealing with bullies, perseverance, the joy of reading and telling stories and the happiness gained from having friends.

A Friend for Little Bear
by Harry Horse

Little Bear lives all alone on a desert island. He wishes he had something to play with. Then a stick comes floating by, followed by a bottle and then a wooden horse. Little Bear and wooden horse play together and have a wonderful time. But problems arise as more and more things come floating by. Finally when he gets a cup the wooden horse falls back into the sea. Bear realises that he doesn't need all these things, that the only thing he really needs is his friend. Enchanting illustrations and a thought provoking story make this a great book to share with children and to discuss possessions, friendship and sharing.

❖✦ All Kinds of Bodies
by Emma Brownjohn

Do you like the way you look? Would you rather look like someone else? Maybe you are large and your best friend is thin. Maybe you have a round face and short neck and another friend has a square face and long neck. Maybe you use a wheelchair or a stick to get around, or wear glasses or a hearing-aid. This delightful lift-the-flap book says that no matter how we look on the outside, under the skin we are all the same – special. An ideal book to encourage children to think about their differences, and similarities, and realise that they are all special, just the way they are.

All Kinds of Feelings
by Emma Brownjohn

Everyone experiences different feelings all of the time. One minute you may feel happy, and another sad or confused. One minute you may feel excited and later bored or lazy. This delightful lift-the-flap book says that it's all right to accept and trust your feelings and to express them. It also points out that it's good to think why we feel a certain way, and whether that is fair.

All Kinds of People
by Emma Damon

This is another attractive lift-the-flap book, which celebrates all kinds of children in a warm and humourous way. It will trigger discussions about the fact that people come in all sorts of different shapes and sizes and have different interests and hobbies. At the end is a mirror and a page to record one's own special characteristics – an exercise that could be extended to every child in the class. This is an excellent resource for raising the notion that different doesn't mean inferior or worse, that individuality is what makes people interesting and that differences manifest themselves in a number of ways.

A Special Something
by Jane Fearnley

A little girl is trying to find out what is in mummy's 'big fat tummy'. She makes all sorts of wild guesses and gets very worried about the effect the 'special something' will have on her life - until all is revealed and she gets to hold her baby brother. Jane Fearnley approaches this difficult subject in a subtle but entertaining way that allows the child to explore and become involved with the physical effects of pregnancy on their mother. It encourages the child to listen to the noises in their mother's stomach, to feel the baby's kicks and movements whilst also exploring the fears they may have about what might be in there and how it will disrupt their lives. All of this is achieved with delightful illustrations and a text that races along and gives the opportunity for some great sound effects!

Baby on Board
by Kes Gray, Sarah Nayler

This story written in language that children will understand about the development of a baby in a mummy's tummy, through to the birth. 'There's a baby growing in Mum's tum. At one month, he's just a blob, at two months, he's half a piece of chewing gum long, and at three months he's as big as mum's thumb.' The pages grow in size as the baby grows each month. The book also talks about the changes in mum – her morning sickness, her love of pickled onions, the baby kicking, getting ready for hospital, and even mum buying bigger bras and knickers! The book is packed with humour, insights into family life and facts about the developing baby. A great book to read with children to promote discussion and understanding of pregnancy, and to talk about their feelings about the birth of siblings.

Badger's Bad Mood
by Hiawyn Oram, Susan Varley

Badger is in a bad mood. He won't see or talk to anyone. The animals are at a loss without him. Who will help with holiday arrangements, give advice and support, take them fishing? Only Mole has the sensitivity to see what is wrong. He secretly organises an award ceremony at which all the animals receive a certificate of achievement. But the real climax of the celebrations is when Badger receives the best award of all. This story tells us all how important it is to tell people you care for them and to appreciate what they do.

Badger's Parting Gifts
by Susan Varley

Badger is dependable, and always ready to lend a helping paw. He is also very old and wise, and knows almost everything. This book is about coming to terms with the death of loved ones. This book is wonderful to share with a child who has suffered a bereavement - it would be best read with that child or a small group of children. Be warned, it is a book that really touches the emotions - read it before you read it aloud to the children in case it touches you too.

Big Book of Families
by Catherine and Lawrence Anholt

'We're all part of that one great big family tree, with branches stretching into towns and villages and cities all over this wonderful planet. Big or small, happy or sad, we all need families.' This book of poems and rhyming text, with detailed illustrations, is a celebration of families, which children will enjoy sharing. Each page contains words and pictures which could evoke children's thoughts and feelings about their own experiences of their families and help them to talk about them.

Big Bird and Little Bird
by Kay Widdowson

Little Bird is too little to do all the things that Big Bird can do - but he tries and tries and finally succeeds. This fun pop-up book says to children that it's the trying that counts. A fun book, full of colourful illustrations of animals that just jump out of the page at you. This is a great book for encouraging children to stop thinking 'I can't' and make them realise that if they persevere with something soon they will be saying 'I can!'

Billy and the Big New School
by Catherine and Lawrence Anholt

A touching and delightful insight into a child's anxieties about starting school. This beautiful story uses the analogy of a little bird, which is picked on by other birds and is cared for by Billy until he is strong enough to fly away. Billy is worried about starting school, feeling nervous, anxious and going off his food. He worries about a range of things - that he won't be able to tie his shoelaces, that he might cry - but soon he is making friends and enjoying school. Billy's situation gives children an opportunity to talk about their worries and anxieties, about overcoming them, and discovering that things they are not looking forward to can turn out to be fun.

Billywise
by Judith Nicholls, Jason Cockcroft

A lyrically told story of the hatching of a little owl chick and his first major challenge, overcoming his fears and learning to fly. Wonderfully atmospheric illustrations and a poetic text make this a book which children will enjoy. The little owl is not sure that he can or will dare to fly, but his mother tells him, 'If you tried, you could glide! Spread your wings to the side, fix your ears on the night, let the stars light your flight and aim for the moon!' A story to build confidence and encourage children have a go, reach for the moon and achieve their dreams. An inspirational tale.

Bored Claude
by Jill Newton

Claude the shark is feeling gloomy. His friends are all very busy but Claude is definitely not interested in what they want to do - it's boring! Back in his cave, feeling crosser than ever, Claude suddenly has a brilliant idea. Maybe there is something they can enjoy together - it just happens to be a little bit different A flamboyant text about friendship and individuality, accompanied by wonderfully energetic art.

Crocodile's Masterpiece
by Max Velthujis

Crocodile is a great artist but he's not managed to sell many paintings. So when Elephant moves in next door and wants to buy one, Crocodile is delighted. But Elephant can't decide which one he'd like, so Crocodile promises to paint him a special picture. This is a thought provoking book, as Elephant discovers that he can close his eyes and enjoy the vision of what ever he wishes for appearing before his eyes. A book to encourage us to dream and see wonder in simple things.

David Gets into Trouble
by David Shannon

When David gets into trouble he always says, 'No. It's not my fault!' He doesn't really mean to get into trouble, most of the time it's just an accident. Sometimes it is his fault, and still he tries to say it wasn't him. Then one night in bed guilt gets the better of him, and frightened he wakes up shouting,'Yes, it was me!' When he apologises his Mum is there to cuddle him and he falls happily back to sleep. Another brilliant David book. Children will love to talk about all the things that he does wrong, and will tell you how they could help him be good.

David Goes to School
by David Shannon

Another beautifully illustrated book about David. This time he is at school and still just as naughty, but he is still loved. Great for getting children to talk about the rules at school (they of course would never do anything as naughty as the things David does! They will probably have lots of ideas to help him behave). David's teacher has her hands full. From running in the corridors to chewing gum in the class, David's high energy antics fill each school day with trouble! In the end though he does say 'Sorry', he cleans up the mess he's made, and the teacher gives him a star for the brilliant job he does at cleaning. A positive note to end on - every child has something they do well!

◆✦ Dr Dog
by Babette Cole

Great illustrations in another fun book which touches on delicate subjects in a witty and non threatening way. The story is about a family and their doctor, who is a dog. It tackles the health issues of smoking, colds, tonsillitis, nits, worms, earache, wind and stress! It will open up lots of discussion about health and looking after ourselves. A word of caution - the page containing the phrase 'he farted so hard he blew the roof off the house!' and the illustration of the toilet flying out of the roof may cause so much hilarity with some children that they may forget the rest of the story and all the previous good advice on keeping healthy! Read it yourself before you read it to children.

Don't Be Horrid, Henry
by Francesca Simon, Kevin McAleenan

It's a dreadful shock for Horrid Henry when Perfect Peter is born, and despite his best - or worst - efforts, he can't manage to get rid of him. As Peter gets bigger, Henry gets crosser. But the day comes when Henry inadvertently finds himself saving Peter from a big fierce dog, and discovers that it's rather nice to be a hero. Plenty of opportunities for children to talk about how Henry could have been a kinder brother, and to talk about their relationships with their own siblings.

Don't Let Go
by Jeanne Willis, Tony Ross

This book is about a little girl who struggles to learn to ride her bicycle. Her father helps her and encourages her, and at last with this support she achieves it. Many of the children in school will be able to relate to how difficult it can be to learn to ride their bikes, but this story should inspire them to understand that if they keep going on most things they can succeed.

◆➤ Excuse Me!
by Lisa Kopelke

Children will laugh and enjoy this book about the frog who burps! But they will discover, as the frog does, that good manners can go a long way and that disgusting habits can lose you friends. Great illustrations and a funny text about a matter that children will relate to! There are plenty of opportunities to bring up discussions about what is rude, what is acceptable behaviour – and whether what is acceptable in one situation might not be in another.

Five Little Fiends
by Sarah Dyer

The five little fiends in the story live inside statues and look out at the world. They each choose a part of the world, their favourite individual part, and take it home, back to their statues to look at whenever they choose. The sun, the moon, the land, the sky and the sea are all removed and stowed away in the statues. Read the story and find out what happens, when each little fiend realises the global impact of his or her combined selfishness. A wonderful picture book about the pleasure of sharing and the beauty of the earth, which The Sunday Telegraph called 'An unsanctimonious ecological parable about greed and sharing'.

Fran's Friend
by Lisa Bruce, Rosalind Beardshaw

A heart warming story about friendship. The short and simple text makes this a lovely story to share with young children, who will also love the bright illustrations. Fran's friend is a dog. He wants to play, but she says she's busy. The dog is sad, upset and goes to his bed, but the story has a happy ending, Fran's been busy making him a card, and in the end they go out to play together. Lots of opportunities to talk about friendship, and also about feeling rejected, sad and lonely, misinterpreting what's going on, and being able to have friendships with and feelings for animals as well as people.

Frog
by Susan Cooper, Jane Browne

Little Joe can't swim and can only sit and watch while his family play in the pool. Then he sees a lost frog leap into the pool. As his family panic - splashing, shouting and screaming while they try to catch the frightened little frog - Joe gently lifts it to safety and sets it free. Watching the frog has given him courage to overcome his own fear. A story about kindness, fear, courage and friendship.

Frog and the Stranger
by Max Velthuijs

When a rat comes to live at the edge of their wood, most of the animals reject him. But Frog, who is friendly by nature, decides to find out if Rat is really as unpleasant as he is made out to be. As he discovers, Rat is intelligent and good-hearted after all, and a true friend in emergencies. This book makes us think about the way we sometimes judge people before we have really got to know them. We all need to follow the example set by Frog.

Frog and the Treasure
by Max Velthuijs

Another tale about this lovable frog, who this time decides to dig for treasure and promises Little Bear they will find some! Frog digs and digs in his search, and eventually both of them end up stuck at the bottom of the hole. Eventually they are rescued by their friends, but Frog is sad and disappointed he feels he has let Little Bear down. However, all is well in the end as he finds that he can, after all, keep his promise. This book makes an excellent introduction to talking about keeping your word and not letting people down – and the pressures this sometimes creates.

Frog Finds a Friend
by Max Velthuijs

Another lovely story about your favourite frog! Here he meets a teddy bear, whom he befriends. He teaches him to talk, takes him for walks, feeds him and shows him friendship and kindness. They do everything together and they become the best of friends. One day the little bear says he has to go away and frog is inconsolable. But the story has a happy ending and the bear returns. A story to get the children talking about friendship, kindness and what it feels like if we loose a friend.

Frog is Hero
by Max Velthuijs

Frog loves the rain, but it doesn't seem much fun when he and his friends are flooded out. Only Hare's house is safe and dry, but Frog, Duck and Pig cannot shelter there forever because their food is running out. As Frog ventures out to fetch more supplies the waters threaten to carry him away. This is a delightful book which will get children thinking and talking about bravery, courage, and pride. A story about helping your friends.

Giraffes Can't Dance
by Giles Andreae, Guy Parker-Rees

This funny, touching and triumphant story is written in rhyming verse, which begs to be read aloud. The preface tells us that the story was written after the author went to Kenya and was struck by the giraffe's gracefulness. 'This led me to thinking that we can all do things which others don't expect us to. All we need is a little encouragement.' Gerald, the giraffe in the story, always dreaded the Jungle Dance, until one beautiful, moonlit night he discovers that 'when we're different sometimes all we need is a different song to dance to...'.

Green Poems
by Jill Bennett

The blurb at the back of the book reads, 'Here's a collection of poems about seeds, fruit, flowers, birds, insects, fish, mammals - and you and me. We all live on the same planet, under the same light, under the same sun. So let's all take care of each other as life goes slowly round and round on Natures strange and amazing ground.' A collection of fantastic poems that you can dip into. Each will evoke some discussion of the world around us, and hopefully encourage us to appreciate it and look after it.

Good Baby, Bad Baby
by Nanette Newman

There are two complete stories here in one back to back book. Start from one end of the story and the baby is good, and start from the other end and the same baby is up to all sorts of mischief! There is a lot to discuss - no one is perfect, we all have good bits and not so good bits, sometimes we show one side, sometimes another. This books is good for getting children to consider all their better qualities, and for talking about what exactly constitutes naughty behaviour, and how people feel when they're on the receiving end of it.

Good Days, Bad Days
Catherine and Lawrence Anholt

Children will love sharing and talking about this brilliant and evocative story of the ups and downs of family life. A simple text is enhance by beautiful pictures, inspired by the authors' own family. The children will relate the experiences to their own, because we all have good days and bad days, and it does us good to talk about them and the way we feel about them.

Goodbye, Mousie
by Robie Harris, Jan Ormerod

When a little boy is told that his pet mouse has died, at first he can't believe it. 'Mousie is NOT dead!' he cries. 'He's just...very...very sleepy this morning.' It is going to take time for him to understand that Mousie really is dead and he's not coming back. With the help of his family, he finds out that it's perfectly OK to feel angry and sad when the pet he loves dies. By voicing his feelings and asking lots of questions, he finally begins to accept Mousie's death. Goodbye Mousie is a perfect book to help children cope with loss.

Guess How Much I Love You
by Sam McBratney, Anita Jeram

In Guess How Much I Love You, a young rabbit named Little Nutbrown Hare thinks he's found a way to measure the boundaries of love. In a heartwarming twist on the 'I-can-do-anything-you-can-do-better' theme, Little Nutbrown Hare goes through a series of declarations regarding the depth of his love for Big Nutbrown Hare. But even when his feelings stretch as long as his arms, or as high as his hops, Little Nutbrown Hare is fondly one-upped by the elder rabbit's more expansive love. This book focuses on love and is excellent for helping children to talk about their affections and feelings.

Hair in Funny Places
by Babette Cole

This is an amusing look at a sensitive subject, more suitable for children in upper Key Stage 2 who have Sex Education. It tackles the subject of bodily growth in a different way, described by The Times as 'an icebreaker that will turn embarrassed giggles into proper laughter.' In this wise but wildly funny, and fantastically illustrated story Cole explains how Mr and Mrs Hormone mix outrageous potions that turn children into adults. Not only does the book talk about the physical changes that the child will experience, growing hair in funny places, periods, etc., but it also addresses the different feelings they will face. This is the best sex education story book I have found, which has also worked with teenagers. However, be sure to read it yourself before you read it to your children.

Have You Seen Elvis?
by Andrew Murray, Nicola Slater

Buddy the dog and Elvis the cat are always fighting, and although Elvis is brave, Buddy is bigger. Elvis has had enough and leaves one night through the cat flap.

Lucy's tears and puffy eyes make Buddy feel so bad that he decides to go and search for his old adversary. But night is a cat's world all right! This is a book packed with pathos, action and humour, which will strike a chord with all feuding children. A great book to read to children who are frequently quarrelling or fighting. With luck maybe they will see that they could lose their friends and that life would be happier if they got along together!

Hoot and Holler
by Alan Brown, Rimantas Rolia

Hoot is a very small owl and Holler a much bigger one. Every night they play together in the Great Wood. They love each other very much, but Hoot is too little to say so and Holler is just too shy. One night a great storm blows them to opposite ends of the wood. Hoot cannot find Holler and Holler cannot find Hoot. Wise Owl's advice gives them the courage to find each other and makes them realise how important it is to tell a friend just how you feel. A beautifully illustrated book about shyness, bravery, and the importance of having the courage to tell friends how you feel.

Home Before Dark
by Ian Beck

When Lily drops Teddy in the park one rainy day, he gets left behind. It's not easy being a little lost teddy, cold and far from home. But Lily can't go to bed without him. Teddy must get home before dark. The book follows Teddy's journey home. Lots of opportunities to talk about being scared, being brave, and personal safety, not going off alone, knowing what to do if we were in danger, lost, or in trouble.

I Don't Care!
by Brian Moses

The theme of this book is learning about respect, and taking care of things that belong to other people – and that includes their feelings! Are you careful with a friend's bike - do you treat it with respect or would you return it battered and broken? Do you take notice of rules or do you just ignore them? Full of everyday situations like these, this book helps us think about being considerate and thinking about the needs and feelings of others. Although it's not a story, the illustrations will make the book very appealing to children and the situations are ones they will be sure to identify with. At the back of the book there are useful notes for teachers.

I Feel Happy
by Mary Murphy

As the title suggests, this book deals with emotions in a context to which very young children can relate. Nobody feels happy all the time! Join Milo, a little dog and his friend, Ellie, as they discover what makes them happy, sad, and angry. I Feel Happy is an ideal book to use with children in the Foundation Stage and

Nurture groups, who will easily identify with the two characters. If you are looking for a resource that you can use to introduce children to talking about feelings, this book will make an ideal start.

I Love You, Blue Kangaroo
by Emma Chichester Clark

Blue Kangaroo is Lily's favourite toy animal and every night he sleeps very well, cuddled up with her. But when Lily is given new animals there just doesn't seem to be enough room for Blue Kangaroo any more. Every night Lily says, 'I love you Blue Kangaroo' and he falls asleep in her arms. But when wild brown bear arrives there is not so much room in the bed for Blue Kangaroo. Lily is also given a yellow cotton rabbit and he joins them in bed, soon to be followed by two furry puppies, a wiggly green crocodile and a host of other animals. One night the bed is just so full that when Lily rolls over Blue Kangaroo falls out. He decides that there is just not enough room for him any more and so he goes to sleep in baby's bed. The next day Lily looks everywhere for Blue Kangaroo and offers the baby all her other animals in exchange for her oldest and favourite toy. A wonderful story about love.

I'll Always Love You
by Peony Lewis

Alex Bear has broken his mother's favourite honey bowl. It was an accident, but he knows she will be cross. 'Will you only love me if I'm good?' he asks her. 'I'll always love you,' she replies. Alex tells his Mum he is sorry he broke the bowl and makes her a new special bowl. The books tells us a story about unconditional love, saying sorry, and forgiveness.

I'm Lonely
by Brian Moses

A book that describes the emotion of loneliness as experienced by young children. Readers will be able to identify with the inventive depictions of what it is like to be lonely and will be inspired by the various solutions on offer. The last page of the book poses the question, 'Perhaps you might know someone who might be feeling Lonely? What could you do to help?' This opens up a good discussion with children and shows them that their actions can influence how others feel. The book also has a section at the back with further ideas for teachers.

I'm Not Invited
by Diana Cain Bluthenthal

There's a party at Charles's house on Saturday, and his friend Minnie hasn't received an invitation. As the week goes on she feels unhappily left out. Charles and Minnie are the best of friends. Charles even names his mealworm after her! So why doesn't he invite Minnie to the party? Minnie spends the week hoping to get an invitation, growing more and more despondent as it doesn't arrive. Sad and angry, she feels very left out, until the day of the party arrives and she discovers the truth at last. The party was Charles sister's party, and Charles didn't want to go. He wanted to play with his friend Minnie. If only Minnie had told her friend how she was feeling, he could have reassured her that they were the best of friends.

I'm Not Your Friend
by Sam McBratney, Kim Lewis

When a little fox's mother says it is getting too late to play, he decides that he's not going to be friends with her anymore. But as the daylight fades and the shadows draw in, the little fox wonders whether it wouldn't be such a bad idea to stay friends with his mother. She carries him back to the safety of their den, out of reach of all the horrible things that might be waiting for him in the dark, and he is very glad to hear that she'll be his friend for ever. A beautifully illustrated book, that leads to reflection on friendship, love and fear.

I'm Sorry
by Sam McBratney, Jennifer Eachus

The two best friends in this story love to play together. But one day things go wrong, they shout at each other and then they don't speak at all. They are both good at pretending that they don't care about having to play on their own now. Perhaps if they could just say 'sorry' everything would be good again – but somebody has to start. This is an exploration of the nature of friendship and the relationship between two toddlers who spend all their time playing together, and then have their first fight. McBratney captures the emotions of the children with a few well-chosen, thought-provoking words that hit straight to the heart of the matter, reminding the reader that no matter what happens, true friends stick together in the end.

⬦ I'm Special
by Jen Green, Mike Gordon

This book focuses on three common types of disability: the inability to walk, blindness and deafness, and shows with sensitivity and gentle humour the day to day experiences of disabled children. There are useful notes at the back for teachers, with suggestions of ways to promote an understanding of disability through discussion and role play. Not really a story book, but the illustrations will make children look at the book as if it is a story. The book concludes with the very important words, 'Everyone is different and special, just like me.'

⬦ I've Got Nits
by Mike Brownlow

This book deals with the itchy subject of nits with humour and knowledge. The book tells children how nits will spread if they share hats, scarves and combs. It tells them the importance of the whole family and class treating their hair to get rid of the nits, and stresses that treatment needs to repeated to make sure that the nits have gone. A fun book, which attaches no stigma to getting nits, saying that they like clean hair and simply are an annoying little insect that exists rather too frequently in children's hair! Clear illustrations show the family dealing with their problem.

I Will Not Ever Never Eat a Tomato
by Lauren Child

Peas, carrots, potatoes, fishfingers and tomatoes - Lola hates them all! There are lots of pictures of food for children to talk about, discussing what they like and what they don't. There is also the importance of keeping an open mind and being prepared to try. Can the children come up with some inventive ways of trying some of the things they say they don't like. The story is fun, with great illustrations. It can be used to spark off discussions about fussy eaters and healthy food, about likes and dislikes and about being open to new ideas.

Is That What Friends Do?
by Marjorie Newman, Peter Bowman

Monkey and Elephant are both alone so they decide to be friends. Monkey has lots of experience of friendship, but Elephant has none. Monkey soon takes charge and has Elephant doing all the things he, Monkey, likes doing best. Poor Elephant doesn't enjoy it nearly as much and eventually goes back to being alone. Can Monkey work out where he has gone wrong so they can be friends again? Marjorie Newman's strong, simple text, brought to life by Peter Bowman's humourous illustrations, confronts and explores one of the key issues of early childhood in a warm and reassuring way. Ideal for young children taking their first steps into the tricky area of friendship.

It Was You, Blue Kangaroo
by Emma Chichester Clark

Lily and Blue Kangaroo are inseparable. Whatever Lily does, Blue Kangaroo does too. But Lily is not always fair, and when she is naughty it is Blue Kangaroo who gets the blame. One day Lily is very bad indeed, and Blue Kangaroo is taken away from her and placed on a shelf downstairs until he learns to behave. But will he? In the middle of the night Blue Kangaroo hops down from the shelf, draws a special picture saying 'sorry' and slips it under Lily's mum's door. Lily's Mum wants to know who drew the lovely picture. And Lily whispers, 'It was you, Blue Kangaroo!' This book addresses issues of love, honesty and unkindness in a sensitive and thought-provoking way.

➻ Jennifer Jones Won't Leave Me Alone
by Frieda Wishinsky, Neal Layton

Written in the first person, this witty, rhyming text is about a little boy who is fed up with the loving attentions of the girl who sits next to him in class. But when the girl in question, Jennifer Jones, goes away he realises how much he misses her and he's the one buying red hearts at the store. A book that will make children laugh, and think about how they react to peers of the opposite sex. There's a great page when the boy knows Jennifer is coming home and his friends want to know why he's excited. 'Should I Lie?' he thinks. What would the children do?

Jonathan Livingston Seagull
by Richard Bach, Russell Munson

Jonathan Livingston Seagull, the most celebrated inspirational fable of our time, tells the story of a bird determined to be more than ordinary. This best-selling modern classic is a story for people who want to follow their dreams and make their own rules and has inspired people for decades. 'Most gulls don't bother to learn more than the simplest facts of flight - how to get from shore to food and back again,' writes author Richard Bach in this allegory about a unique bird named Jonathan Livingston Seagull. 'For most gulls it is not flying that matters, but eating. For this gull, though, it was not eating that mattered, but flight.' Flight is indeed the metaphor that makes this story soar. Ultimately, he learns the meaning of love and kindness.

Just Like You
by Jan Fearnley

This is a very appealing book. The drawings are wonderful and the text flows beautifully. The story introduces children to the concept that all animal parents (yes, there's a reference to a daddy frog who's looking after his froglets) love their animal children... therefore so do we humans. The story ends with mama mouse tiptoeing out of the room as baby mouse goes to sleep in the knowledge that they are both very special. This is a perfect book for children who are anxious and may need some reassurance that they are loved and that they are special.

Kitty Princess and the Newspaper Dress
by Trevor Dickinson, Emma Carlow

Kitty Princess thinks she is the prettiest princess in town - but actually she is the rudest! She never says please, thank you or sorry. After being rude to her fairy godmother, Kitty sets off to town to find her own outfit for the ball. But she soon learns that being rude to people doesn't get her very far, and in the end she learns to say sorry. Exuberant illustrations and an enjoyable story make this a book children enjoy. At first they feel amused by Kitty and her rudeness, but they soon realise that her behaviour doesn't get her what she wants and reach the conclusion that it doesn't pay to be unpleasant to people. This story makes a great introduction to talking about the importance of good manners and polite words.

L is for Loving
by Ken Wilson-max

An ABC for the way you feel. This bold, exuberant and colourful picture book shows an emotion for every letter of the alphabet and captures twenty six emotions and feelings from angelic to zippy. A great book for looking at the wide range of emotions we can feel. Challenge children to think of more emotions for each letter.

Letters Around the World
by Thando Maclaren

This lovely book has a series of letters which you can take out of their envelopes and share with the children. These letters from pen-pals describe how children live in other countries - their families, their favourite food, hobbies and special celebrations. The book includes letters from children in India, Tanzania, New Zealand, Trinidad and Indonesia. A book to promote discussion about different customs, different lives, different countries.

Lilly's Purple Plastic Purse
by Kevin Henkes

Lily gets into trouble with her teacher because she keeps playing with her brand new plastic purse at school. She learns about commitment, apologies, and controlling her temper, and the importance of deferred gratification. A wonderful story about Lily who brings to school a special purse and can't wait to show it to the class. She doesn't listen to her teacher and when he takes it off her she decides she no longer likes him! In her temper she draws a nasty picture of him. On her way home she finds he has left something in the purse for her and she realises she has a special teacher. She's sorry and apologises to him. Discussion of being angry, being wrong, admitting mistakes and saying sorry can all arise from this book.

Little Beaver and the Echo
by Amy Macdonald, Sarah Fox-Davies

Little Beaver lives all alone by the edge of the pond. He has no family and he has no friends. He's a very sad and lonely little beaver. But one day, when he starts to cry, he hears someone else crying too, on the other side of the pond. So begins his touching quest for a friend. This is a book for children to enjoy, which will inspire discussion about how we feel without friends and how, as you offer friendship, so too you find it yourself.

Little Snail's Big Surprise
Carla Dijs

A lively, exciting book which will engage and stimulate young children. This charming story really captures and engages young minds. It tells of Little Snail guessing what his big surprise might be. In the end he finds out that it is a new baby brother and sister. The book encourages children to talk about their feelings when younger siblings arrive. Is it a 'Big Surprise' for them when they discover a that there's a new member of the family? Although about the birth of siblings, the story could also be used to initiate discussion about any additions to the family, including those which come about through a parent's new partnership.

Lost: One Dog, Green
by Pascal Biet

Sometimes being different can make life a tricky, but instead of hiding away it is often best to go out and face the world, where you are likely to discover that being different is not so bad after all. This theme is explored through the story of Sarah and her dog, James, who is extraordinarily green. She is worried that if she lets James out the other dogs in the neighbourhood will pick on him because he is different, but James gets bored staying indoors and decides to venture out. He is quickly confronted by a gang of dogs, but instead of picking on him they are full of admiration for his wonderful green colouring. This gives James a marvellous idea, so he sets to work colouring all the dogs and soon there are pink dogs, orange dogs, blue dogs and even multi-coloured stripy dogs. Sarah is delighted. Finally she and James are able to go to the park without fear of being picked on.

Martha's Friends
by Emma Damon

Martha is very shy until a bully comes to school, when she finds her voice, and lots of friends. A brilliant lift-the-flap book to use when talking to children about being shy, bullying, and what they should do if they feel bullied. Matha makes the telling point, 'Don't you know that everyone is different?' to the bully.

Mine!
by Hiawyn Oram, Mary Rees

This cautionary tale provides a valuable lesson to all children. The perils of visiting your best friend and expecting to play with her toys are well described in a wonderfully simple manner. Isabel visits her friend Claudia and discovers she is less than willing to share any of her belongings. A pacifying move by mum, by taking them to the park, back-fires slightly when Claudia's new tricycle takes a disastrous trip of its own, providing us with a witty tour through the park and ending with a great punch line and valuable moral. This book offers a great lesson on sharing.

Mole and the Baby Bird
by Marjorie Newman, Patrick Benson

A touching story about a little mole that discovers a baby bird which has fallen out of its nest. He takes it home and it soon recovers after some loving attention. Inevitably, nature is stronger than Mole's well-meaning care, and once the bird regains its strength it attempts to fly for the first time. Mole is alarmed by this and builds a cage to contain the bird, despite his parents' warnings that it's not meant to be kept as a pet. It takes a visit from Mole's grandad for him to realise that sometimes the kindest thing you can do for something you love is to let it be free. A book about caring and kindness which can also be used to talk with children about looking after animals and the world around them.

Mouse, Mole and the Falling Star
by A.H. Benjamin, John Bendall-Brunello

Mole and Mouse are the best of friends. They share everything together and trust each other completely. Then one day they see a falling star. Instead of sharing, they start to quarrel over who saw the star first and they are torn apart. But they soon begin to miss each other. Ultimately they realise that they would rather have each other than have the star – 'Anyway, we don't need a star. We have each other,' says mouse, and Mole agrees. A heartwarming story about the importance of friends and friendship.

My Friend Bear
by Jez Alborough

Eddy and the bear are both feeling sad. They both wish they had a friend to talk to, but they only have their teddies - and teddies can't talk. Or can they? A misunderstanding leads to a game of ventriloquism, which in turn leads to the forming of a friendship. A beautifully illustrated book which will encourage children to talk about feelings of loneliness, and how it doesn't matter if your friend is different from you. A book that shows the joy of friendship.

My Nose, Your Nose
by Melanie Walsh

'Arthur's nose turns up. Agnes's nose turns down. But they both like the smell of chocolate cake!' Bright, bold illustrations and a clear, simple text, encourage children to think about the differences and similarities between people in this celebration of individuality. A great book for younger children to enjoy, and to get them looking at the differences and similarities between each other.

No, David!
by David Shannon

A wonderfully child-like book that really draws young listeners in. Poor David! He always seems to be at the end of a strong 'NO David!!!' He is just a typical boy, surrounded by adults and their rules that just don't seem important to him. In the end the children learn that even though David is often told off, he is reassured that his mother does love him. This is especially reassuring to little ones who have to fight for places in their parent's busy schedules. They may indeed hear the word 'no' much more than any other. It ends on a very positive note. It shows them that the mother in the book still loves her little naughty boy.

◆→ No Matter What
Debi Gliori

An excellent book in every way, containing beautiful illustrations, simple rhyming phrases and a moving storyline. It is a simple but funny story of a mother fox's affirmation to her young cub of her unconditional love, and of how she sets her cub's mind at rest about all his worries. Although the main theme is love, this lovely book also touches on death in the question, 'But what about when we're dead and gone, would you love me then, does love go on?' The story reassures us that love never dies. 'The literary equivalent of a Big Hug!' The Times.

One World
by Michael Foreman

This powerful story will make children think about looking after the environment, and about how the smallest part of that environment is part of a bigger world to which we all belong. Some children are playing in a rock pool on the beach. 'The pool, which had reminded the children of the beauty of the world, now showed how easily it could be spoiled. It reminded them of the larger world they knew where forests were disappearing in clouds of smoke and people in towns were poisoning the land and seas. Atmospheric illustrations and an evocative text make this a great book to provoke discussion on looking after the world around us.

◆→ Petar's Song
by Pratima Mitchell, Caroline Binch

A story about the impact of war and the pain caused by family separation. When Petar, his mother, brother and sister have to leave their valley and cross the border for safety, leaving their father behind, Petar no longer feels like playing his violin. He misses his father so much he doesn't feel like celebrating Christmas and feels he will never be happy again. One day as he thinks of his father a new song enters his head, a song of peace, and soon he plays his violin again and brings joy and hope to those around him. There are plenty of opportunities here to talk about happiness and sadness, pleasure and pain, and how these feelings can affect you.

Princess Snooty-cat
by Emma Damon

Princess Moonbeam seems to have everything - a huge palace and hundreds of dresses. But when she goes to town in her stretch limousine, no one comes out to greet her. She is determined to find out why she is so unpopular, so she dresses as a cat and cycles back into town. Now she is much more popular. She finally understands that it's better to be friendly to everyone than to be snooty. Princess Moonbeam learns that kindness and good manners helps her make friends, and friends make her happier than anything she can buy. Great pictures and flaps to peep into make this book a winner with children.

Rapunzel
by Lynn and David Roberts

Just such a lovely version of this charming fairy tale, with wonderful illustrations. A great many emotions feature in the story, from the evil and unkind Aunt Edna to Rapunzel herself, lost and lonely in the city, and Roger and Rapunzel's friendship. Maybe the best approach is just to read and enjoy this story, and see where it takes the children in a discussion led by them.

Rainbow Fish to the Rescue!
by Marcus Pfister

Rainbow Fish must choose between his new-found friends and a lonely little fish when a dangerous, hungry shark threatens the reef. It gives the children plenty of stimulation to think and creates great opportunities for them to practice a variety of skills across the curriculum. This is a book that encourages discussions about decisions that can be difficult, when we are faced with peer pressure. Fear, bravery, courage and loneliness are all emotions found within this story.

Really Brave Tim
by John Prater

Billy, Millie and Suki are in Tim's den boasting about how brave they are. Billie boasts about his midnight walk in the woods, Millie describes her underwater adventure and Suki explains why she's not afraid of heights. Poor Tim doesn't feel very brave - he is scared of the dark, he can't swim, and he is afraid of heights. However, he dreams up a hairy, scary way to prove he's the bravest of them all. He finds a spider and all his friends are afraid of it! A lovely story that illustrates our individuality. Sometimes we can all be brave, but sometimes something may frighten us - for each of us it will probably be something different that triggers these emotions.

Rude Mule
by Pamela Duncan Edwards, Barbara Nascimbeni

What would you do if a mule knocked on your door one day and said, 'I've come for lunch.'? You'd say, 'Hello! Come in, Mule.' But what if the mule was badly behaved? Find out how a quick-witted little boy teaches an obstinate mule some manners in this funny, touching picture book. With repetitive dialogue and mule noises to make, this is a great book to read aloud and wonderful to get children talking about being polite and having manners. How would they teach the Mule to behave? Can they make up a story called 'Polite Mule'?

Sitting Duck
by Michael Bedard

A fun, zany story with great pictures, by a now well-known pop artist. The endearing and wacky characters in the story will have children captivated, and the story will provoke a range of different thoughts in children. It could bring up discussion about food, and maybe a topic on factory produced food and farmed food. It could also stimulate thinking about friendships between those we think might be unlikely to be friends. Finally there is material on exercising and leading a more healthy life, to make your life better. And of course, it's a story worth enjoying, just for its own sake.

So Hungry
by Daniel Morden, Suzanne Carpenter

A story about going to bed when you are hungry, and then having a weird and wonderful dream all about food. The story itself is not about healthy eating, but the illustrations are such fun (with a boat made out of a baked potato and pages of bright and zany fruit and vegetables) that it will inspire children to talk about their favourite food, healthy eating, and to create their own wacky pictures using pictures of food. The story could also lead to thinking about famine and starvation, and about people less fortunate than ourselves.

➡ Sophie and the New Baby
by Catherine and Lawrence Anholt

Waiting for a new baby is a very exciting and magical time, but it can also be a difficult experience for older brothers and sisters. For a while the family life they have got used to can be turned upside down. This story can help children understand the mixed feelings they may have about a new arrival in their home and reassure them about the good times that will lie ahead. Beautiful illustrations show the changing seasons of the years as the time goes by and the baby is born, and then grows into a toddler. Endless details for children to discover and talk about.

Tadpole's Promise
by Jeanne Willis, Tony Ross

I first heard this story read by Gervase Phinn, and remember listening intently to every word and the range of emotions I experienced as he read it. Even with lesser story telling skills this tale will evoke many emotions in those who hear or read it. Be warned though, this story doesn't have a happy ending, and there is an unexpected twist in the tale that children rarely encounter in stories. However, many of them will have already learnt from their own experiences that life doesn't always follow the 'and they all lived happily ever after' recipe for an ending. A tale of love and broken promises, this is also a great book to follow up work on life cycles as it follows the life cycle of both the butterfly and the frog. Read it yourself before you read it to children.

➽ The Colour of Home
by Mary Hoffman, Karin Littlewood

This moving story is about a Somalian child starting school in England after fleeing his country. It is very touching and maybe the situation could be a little too close to home for some children. However, for others it might be the spark that encourages them to share their thoughts and experiences. For most children it will be an excellent book to help raise issues such as asylum and immigration. The boy in the story paints pictures of his home, so it could provide an interesting start to a painting session where children are encouraged to think of the feelings that different colours evoke. Read it yourself, before you share it with your class.

The Gossipy Parrot
by Shen Roddie, Michael Terry

Godfrey the gossipy parrot is always passing rude remarks and stirring up trouble. One day Lion decides enough is enough and that he will teach Godfrey a lesson. Children will enjoy the wonderful pictures in this book, from the illustrator of 'The Selfish Crocodile', and the text is simple. It opens up discussion about how sometimes words can cause upset, just as actions can. It teaches us to think before we say something and to refrain from gossiping or saying hurtful things to others.

The Happy Hedgehog
by Marcus Pfister

Mikko, the hedgehog, loved his garden. He knew all the plants and flowers that grew there, and he enjoyed learning about their healing powers. He thought he was perfectly content - until Grandfather Tarek came and told him he was wasting his time. Mikko sets off to see what everyone else is doing. All the creatures he meets are busy and ambitious, working hard to become the fastest, the cleverest or the strongest. Mikko tries to be just like them, though they don't seem to be enjoying life at all, and joining in with them doesn't make Mikko happy. This lovely character shows us that there is more to life than being the best at everything.

➽ The Lion Who Wanted To Love
by Giles Andreae, David Wojtowycz

'You've got to be strong to be different, and when you've got love on your side you've got the most valuable gift that there is.' These words are from the last page of this inspiring book about a little lion who didn't want to fight, and stuck to his convictions and beliefs and showed kindness and friendship to all the animals in the jungle. When faced with danger himself, his friends saved him. A story in rhyming verse, which children will enjoy hearing, and with lively illustrations, this is an excellent resource for encouraging talk about strength, violence and whether might is right. It is also useful for getting boys to think by questioning stereotypical male behaviour, such as aggression, but needs sensitive use.

The Polar Bear and the Snow Cloud
by Jane Cabrera

How can a lonely little polar bear find a friend to play with? This is a tale about a little polar bear looking for a friend but not having much luck. It's not going to be easy, but he won't give up hope. The poor bear is sad but still he doesn't give up, and in the end he finds another polar bear to be his friend. This beautifully illustrated book emphasises the value of determination and persistence. Children enjoy the simple, endearing tale and identify with the little bear and his feelings of loneliness.

The Three Grumpies
by Tamra Wright, Ross Collins

A hilarious picture book for all of us who sometimes find ourselves the victims of grumpy moods! When a little girl wakes up she finds, Grumpy, Grumpier and Grumpiest waiting for her, and they are determined to make her life a misery! When she starts to look on the funny side of the disastrous goings on, things begin to pick up for the little girl. Eventually the Grumpies give up and disappear. This story will help children to realise that when they feel in a grumpy mood, if they try and look on the bright side of things, their mood will soon change and they will feel much better. This is a story to encourage children to talk about their feelings and their moods, and how we can change the way we feel.

The Rainbow Fish
by Marcus Pfister

This story teaches children the benefits of sharing things, rather than being selfish. The Rainbow Fish is handsome, but won't share and feels contempt for other creatures who are not as spectacular. This is a beautifully illustrated book; the fish's shiny silver scales stand out in the pictures and will fascinate children. It has an underlying message of sharing with others and how good this makes people feel. The Rainbow Fish discovers that he is much happier with only one special scale and lots of friends, than he was when he wouldn't share his prized scales.

The Rainbow Fish and the Big Blue Whale
by Marcus Pfister

When a big blue whale comes to live near their reef, there is a misunderstanding between him and Rainbow Fish and his friends that leaves everyone very unhappy and hungry. When Rainbow Fish bravely sets off to make peace with the whale, he discovers that the Whale had been hurt and angry because of the hostile things the fish had been saying. The book shows us that sometimes misunderstandings can escalate into a disagreement which nobody really wants. Talking together can sort our differences out.

❖ The Red Tree
by Shaun Tan

There are brilliant and sumptuously coloured images in this funny and uplifting book. Each picture features a little girl. In many of them she looks unhappy and lost, but in them all, if you look closely, you will see a red leave fluttering somewhere. The leaf represents hope, and no matter how sad and sorry the picture looks there's always hope there. 'Sometimes the day begins with nothing to look forward to…' the book begins, and then goes on to show how it's always possible to find something positive to enjoy and be thankful for. This is an excellent book for discussions and assemblies, but although the text is simple the images are sophisticated and therefore it is best shared with slightly older children.

The Richest Crocodile in the World
by Daniel Postgate

In a crumbly old mansion in Africa lives the richest crocodile in the world. He has everything his heart desires but despite this he is not happy. On his own with all his possessions the crocodile is unhappy, but when he shares what he has and joins his friends 'he's still rich, but in a different way now.' This story deals with a cliché, that money doesn't bring happiness, but it manages to do this without being trite and is sure to provoke discussion about what things make you happy and what don't.

The Selfish Crocodile
by Faustin Charles, Mike Terry

Every morning a very large and very snappy crocodile shouts, 'Stay away from my river! It's MY river! If you come in my river, I'll eat you all!' All the animals are frightened to go in the river until one day the crocodile is ill, and a mouse solves their dilemma. The brave mouse helps take care of the crocodile's teeth and soon they become the best of friends. When the crocodile discovers how much better life is with friends he stops being selfish and invites the other animals to share the river. A book that touches bullying, friendship, sharing and of course looking after your teeth!

The Smartest Giant in Town
by Julia Donaldson, Alex Scheffler

George was very happy being the scruffiest giant in town. But one day, when he sees a shop stocking giant-size clothes, he decides it's time to up-date his image. With smart trousers, a shirt, tie and shiny shoes, George is a new giant. However, as he goes home, he meets various animals who desperately need his help... and his new clothes! Very soon his immaculate wardrobe is devastated. However, there's a plus side. George may no longer be the smartest giant in town, but he's certainly the kindest! Children love this beautifully illustrated book, watching as the giant gives all his smart clothes away to help his friends. The thank you letter from his friends is also good for stressing the importance of children saying thankyou, and can lead to practice in expressing thanks, both orally and in writing.

The Very Lazy Ladybird
by Isobel Finn, Jack Tickle

The very lazy ladybird likes to sleep all day and all night. And because she sleeps all day and all night, she doesn't know how to fly. One day, she decides she wants to sleep somewhere else so she hops onto a kangaroo, but that's too bouncy, the tiger is too noisy, but the elephant's trunk is great … until it sneezes and then the ladybird has to learn to fly! A good book for talking to children about the fact that if you are lazy you don't learn lots of very useful skills!

The World Came To My Place Today
by Jo Readman, Ley Honor Roberts.

George is poorly in bed, and his grandfather tells him he will bring the world to visit him. He brings a globe and then tells the boy about the origins of the food he is eating, and things around him, like the plants that become chocolate, baked beans, rubber tyres, cotton t-shirts and paper for books. I first saw this book at the Eden Project, and already inspired by the place, I thought this was a great story which children would find fascinating as they discover how plants from all over the world affect their daily lives. The Daily Mail calls the book 'A mind expander for a small child.' At the beginning the author writes, 'Enjoy your food, and travel the world with it. Look after the plants that look after you.' A book to inspire a child's knowledge of the world and encourage them to care for it.

Three Cheers For Ostrich
by Francesca Simon, Neal Layton.

A charming story about the importance of being kind and caring towards others. Ostrich feels that all his friends seem to do everything better than he does and he is beginning to think that he isn't very good at anything at all, until his mother points out something very important when she asks who is the kindest. The story will also help spark discussion about boasting, and how our actions can affect the way others feel.

◆◆ Tissue Please!
by Lisa Kopelke

Frog and his friends can't stop sniffing. What's worse, they have no use for tissues and they wipe their noses on their arms! It's making their teacher feel disgusted! (How many teachers know that feeling!) I had to smile as I read the book, and could imagine those children that would listen as you read it and be full of 'eerr, yuk!' comments, and yet be sitting there themselves, sniffling and wiping their noses on their sleeves! Children will laugh and enjoy this humourous and exuberant tale, and hopefully they too will reach for the box of tissues, and then chuck the tissue in the bin when they've used it! Although humourous, this story is good to introduce serious discussions, not only about personal sensibilities but also about health and hygiene.

◆→ Truelove
by Babette Cole

This is another book that touches on a delicate subject, a child's feeling of being ignored when a new baby arrives. In this unique, funny and audacious story a dog called Truelove is ignored when the new baby arrives, despite his many efforts to help. It is only when he leaves home that we are made to realise that true love means forgiveness. A great tale to share with children who may encounter similar feelings when a young sibling enters their life.

◆→ Up in Heaven
by Emma Chichester Clark

This simple tale is about Daisy, who has a pet dog called Authur, who dies. The story is reassuring and refreshingly unsentimental about death. An ideal book to soothe emotions, it opens a door on a difficult subject with elegant tenderness. By dealing openly and directly with the loss felt following the death of a loved person or animal, this book will promote discussion about what happens when someone dies and how we can move on and cope with our feelings of loss. It may also lead to speculation about heaven and the afterlife.

Voices in the Park
by Anthony Browne

Four people go to the park, and through their eyes we see four different versions of what took place there. There's the bossy woman, the sad man, the lonely boy and the young girl whose warmth touches them all. As the story moves from one voice to another, their perspectives are reflected in the shifting landscapes and seasons. Beautifully and imaginatively illustrated, this book encourages us to explore the impact we have on each other, just as the characters in the book influence one another. This is an excellent resource for introducing discussion about the differences between people and the different ways people interpret events. Although some of these concepts are more suitable for older children, there is material here for the younger ones too.

What Colour is Love?
by Linda Strachan, David Wojtowycz.

This book is particularly suitable for younger children. Not only will it offer plenty of stimulation through brilliant and vibrant illustrations, it will also get them discussing love. 'What colour is Love? Every colour, all around, because nothing else matters when it's love that you've found.' Not only will the book encourage children to talk about the things and people that mean a lot to them, but it will also open up discussions about the different feelings that colours can evoke in us all.

What is Peace?
by Emma Damon

Here is another beautifully illustrated, lift-the-flap book, not only suitable for younger children, but also useful in Key Stage 2 as a discussion starting point. The simplicity of the statements and the great pictures could inspire a thought provoking display about what peace means to a child. Some of the illustrations when you lift the flaps are repeated in our copy. I'm not sure if this is a printing error, or intentional, but let the children decide - they no doubt could come up with some more ideas!

Whatever Wanda Wanted
by Jude Wisdom

Wanda is a very spoilt child. With the stamp of her foot the cutest doll or the frilliest frock and even the prettiest kitten is hers, until she becomes stranded on an island. When her friend Bill the whale takes her home she has leant that there is more to life than things! A hilarious cautionary tale about the perils of materialism. The colourful extravagant illustrations, and the witty rhyming words make this a tale which children will love to hear, and they will have a lot to say about Wanda's behaviour.

Where Are You, Blue Kangaroo?
by Emma Chichester Clark

Lily loves Blue Kangaroo, but sometimes he disappears and Lily says, 'Where are you, Blue Kangaroo?' And Blue Kangaroo waits for Lily to find him. When Lily goes to the park she has a great time, but forgets to hold on tight to Blue Kangaroo and nearly loses him. And when Lily goes shopping with Aunt Jemima, she leaves poor Blue Kangaroo on the bus! Luckily he is returned to her, but by now Blue Kangaroo is feeling very anxious. Then one day Lily goes to the zoo with Uncle George and again Blue Kangaroo is nearly lost, but the trip gives him an idea that will mean he will never be lost again. But where, oh where is Blue Kangaroo the very next morning? This charming book deals with love, anxiety and looking after others.

Willy and Hugh
by Anthony Browne

Willy the chimp is lonely. He mooches about, observing the rest of the world having fun. Then an unexpected encounter with huge Hugh changes this as Willy discovers that it is useful to have a friend around. Willy and Hugh are very different but they can both bring something special to their friendship. A book about accepting our differences, bullying, fears and being kind to each other.

With Love
by W. Cooling

This is simply a lovely book for enjoying with young children. Royalties from its sale go to Bookstart, a charity set up to encourage sharing books with babies and nurturing a lifelong love of reading in all children. This alone seems a good enough reason to add this book to our collection.

Who Loves You, Little Beetle?
by Carla Dijs

This is a wonderful story about the importance of being an individual. It's a beautifully illustrated, pop-up book which successfully carries the message of how important it is to remember that we are all individuals. Children who listen to the story should really feel for the main character and they will love the ending. Although the book makes reference to God, it is not linked to any particular religious faith - it is really a book which celebrates the fact that we are all different, but still all special. A very useful resource for assemblies.

Willy the Wizard
by Anthony Browne

Willy loves football but can't afford any boots. He goes to practice every week, but no-one passes him the ball and he's never picked for the team. One night he meets a strange footballing figure who gives him a pair of boots. Willy practices his football skills everyday and he gets picked for the team. But, horror of horrors, on the day of the match he forgets his boots. How will he play without them? Despite the crowd jeering, Willy went on the pitch and did his very best, forgetting that he didn't have his magic boots, and scored the winning goal. This book can be used to explore many issues. Willy is teased and taunted. Willy continues to pursue his dream, and never gives in. The book also touches on daily personal hygiene as Willy cleans his teeth regularly.

You Choose
by Nick Sharratt, Pippa Goodhart

This is a highly interactive book, crammed with colourful illustrations, and marvellous for developing speaking and listening skills. 'If you could go anywhere, where would you go? Who would you like as a friend? How would you travel? And what would you do for fun?' Lots of questions and brilliant illustrations to inspire children to talk. Not a story, just simple text, and wonderful, busy pictures to get children thinking and talking about their choices.

Wanda's First Day
by Mark Sperrings

This is a delicious, funny and beautifully illustrated story about starting school - with a difference! Its Wanda's first day at school, but she discovers that all the other pupils are fairies and she is a witch! At first she's uneasy, but by the end of the day she is enjoying herself so much that she realises it doesn't matter that she's different. This is another great story for opening up thinking about being different, and about why individuality is a treasure, not a curse.

Wonder Goal
by Michael Foreman

This is a tale of a young boy who achieves his dream of becoming a famous footballer. A perfect book for the boys and the football fans, but also a book for everyone else - to encourage us to dream and know that those dreams can come true. It's a book to get children talking about their hopes, an opportunity for them to know that what might seem like an impossible dream, can become reality.

You've Got Dragons
by Kathryn Cave, Nick Maland

Do your worries ever reach dragon-like proportions? The author conveys children's thoughts and feelings with honesty and integrity. This is a brilliant book in which dragons are a metaphor for worries. There is a wonderful page entitled 'Ben's top tips for when you've got dragons'. This would be a great page to look at with children who might be suffering from stress, for example worrying about SATs, or have other concerns. Suitable for use in Key Stage 1 and 2 PSHE classes to inspire discussions relating to confidence and feelings.

Zed the Zebra
by A. Vrombaut

Zed the Zebra is proud of his stripes and is always boasting about how he is the fastest runner in all of Africa. The other animals challenge him to an obstacle race, and Zed is convinced he will win. A similar story to the tale of the Hare and the Tortoise, for in the end when the Zebra is standing admiring the reflection of his stripes all the other animals zoom past him. 'Sometimes you win, and sometimes you lose but at least we all had fun!' We want children to be proud of what they can do, and confident in their abilities, and sometimes it can be hard to know the difference between this and boasting. This book will evoke just such a discussion and get children thinking about how they can express their achievements in a positive way.

Resources

The following pages contain examples of some of the resources we use to support our approach to emotional literacy through books and stories.

Book Cards

We put one of these in the front of each book. We illustrate them with clip-art, but you may wish to get the children to do their own illustrations based on the stories. There are two examples here, and a lot more on the CD.

Word Bank

We use these word cards in a variety of ways to support our work - discussion focuses, word recognition, spelling, labels, etc. You can photocopy the ones here, or print them from the CD.

I Can Statements

We use 'I Can Statements' to talk about, to make posters and to recognise positive behaviour. These are reduced sized versions, with full size ones on the CD.

Word Frames

You may want to make your own book cards. These frames will make attractive borders. They are all on the CD.

Games

Book Cards

These and more are on the CD

Emotional Literacy.

Rude Mule
Pamela Duncan Edwards, Barbara Nascimbeni

What would you do if a mule knocked on your door one day and said, "I've come for lunch."? You'd say, "Hello! Come in, Mule." But what if the mule was badly behaved? Find out how a quick-witted little boy teaches an obstinate mule some manners in this funny, touching picture book. With repetitive dialogue and mule noises to make, this is a great book to read aloud.

A great book to get children to talk about being polite and having manners. How would they teach the Mule to behave? Can they make up a story called "Polite Mule!"

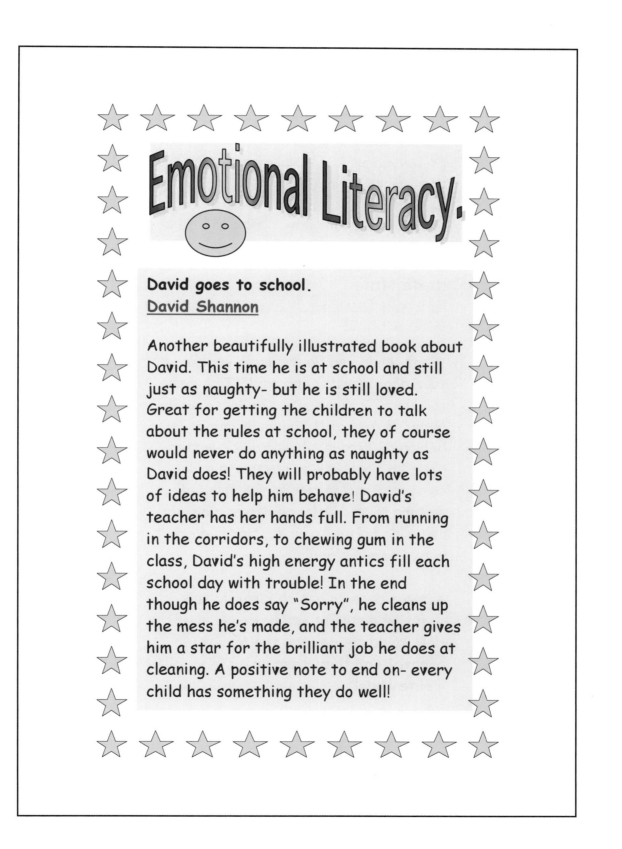

Emotional Literacy.

David goes to school.
David Shannon

Another beautifully illustrated book about David. This time he is at school and still just as naughty- but he is still loved. Great for getting the children to talk about the rules at school, they of course would never do anything as naughty as David does! They will probably have lots of ideas to help him behave! David's teacher has her hands full. From running in the corridors, to chewing gum in the class, David's high energy antics fill each school day with trouble! In the end though he does say "Sorry", he cleans up the mess he's made, and the teacher gives him a star for the brilliant job he does at cleaning. A positive note to end on- every child has something they do well!

Word Bank Cards

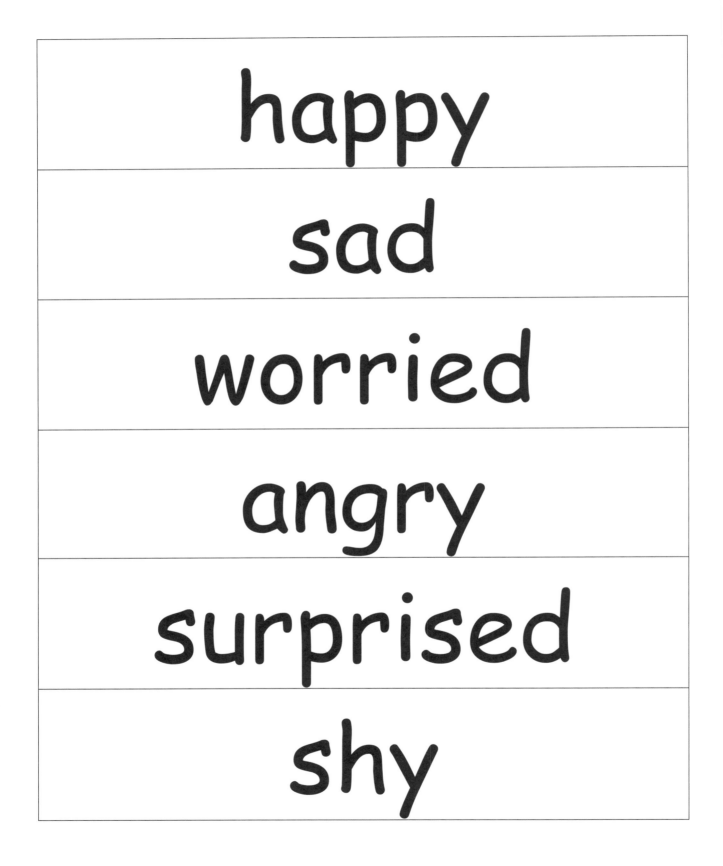

| happy |
| sad |
| worried |
| angry |
| surprised |
| shy |

| tired |
| disappointed |
| cross |
| fit |
| loved |
| excited |

| frightened |
| hurt |
| jealous |
| lonely |
| cheerful |
| proud |
| brave |

'I Can'
Statements

These are on the
CD at full size.

I can say how I feel.

I can say one thing I would like to be better at.

I can share.

'I Can' Statements

These are on the CD at full size.

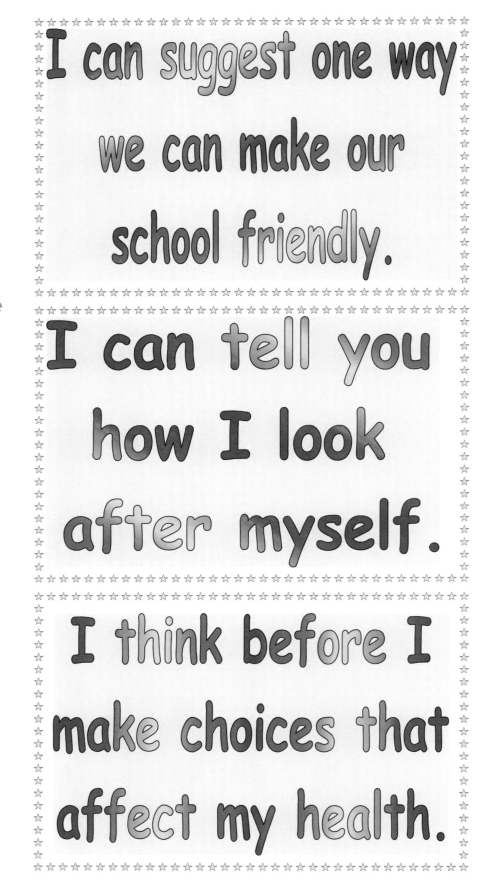

I can suggest one way we can make our school friendly.

I can tell you how I look after myself.

I think before I make choices that affect my health.

'I Can' Statements

These are on the CD at full size.

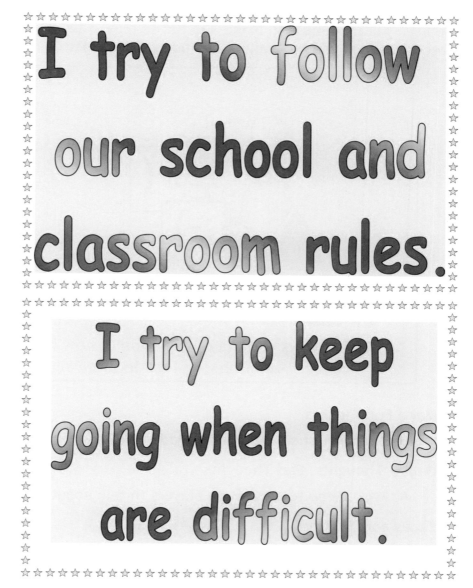

I try to follow our school and classroom rules.

I try to keep going when things are difficult.

The Emotional Literacy Kit

Games are a great way for getting children to talk about feelings. Learning to win and to lose helps them to recognise and understand their own feelings and to appreciate and empathise with the feelings of others. Games encourage turn-taking, fair play, orderly behaviour and the importance of rules.

The following pages contain ideas and instructions for producing games and other resources designed to encourage children to talk about their emotions and feelings. All are simple to make and fun to play. They make use of low cost materials which will be available in most school classrooms and nursery bases.

© 1997 Randy Glasbergen. E-mail: randy@glasbergen.com   www.glasbergen.com

"You always complain that I don't know how to show my emotions, so I made these signs."

1. Make Fun Figures

A collection of simple figures made of card or felt with hundreds of uses.

2. Happy Thoughts, Sad Thoughts

A board game to encourage players to talk about their feelings.

3. Faces and Feelings

Photocopiable outlines of faces for children to draw expressions.

4. One Hundred Square

A 100 square template to use for making up games.

5. Word Frames

Photocopiable frames for you to make your own book cards.

1. Make Fun Figures

Simple figures made of card or felt can be used in lots of ways. The children can draw the outlines and older ones can cut them out with scissors. Try several different sizes. Get the children to colour them, adding clothes, hair and facial expressions. Encourage them to make some young, some old, some male and some female. Many children like to model the figures on their own families.

Make two cut-outs for each figure, so that one can be a front and the other a back. Children can draw a different expression on each side of the figure. Stick Velcro or Blu-Tak on the backs, so that the figures can be used on story boards. Stick on lollipop sticks to make puppets.

Encourage the children to make up stories using the characters they have made. Or to use the figures to 'act out' some of the stories featured in our list.

2. Happy Thoughts, Sad Thoughts

This is a board game to encourage players to talk about their feelings. You need the board, a die and counters.

The game is similar to Snakes and Ladders, but when a player lands on a happy face they share a happy thought or talk about something that makes them happy, and then move up to the 'think' bubble. When they land on a sad face they share a sad thought and move down to the think bubble.

It is important for the children to realise that it doesn't matter who gets to the top square first. The winner is the person who can say a happy thought or a sad thought each time they land on the appropriate face.

The board is on the next page and on the CD. If you have the equipment to print it from the CD on to A3 paper it will be easier to play.

100	99	98	97	96	95	94	93	92	91
81	82	83	84	85	86	87	88	89	90
80	79	78	77	76	75	74	73	72	71
61	62	63	64	65	66	67	68	69	70
60	59	58	57	56	55	54	53	52	51
41	42	43	44	45	46	47	48	49	50
40	39	38	37	36	35	34	33	32	31
21	22	23	24	25	26	27	28	29	30
20	19	18	17	16	15	14	13	12	11
1	2	3	4	5	6	7	8	9	10

Happy thoughts, sad thoughts

When you land on a happy face, say what the happy thought might be and move up the think bubble.

**If you land on the sad face, say what the sad thought might be, and move down the think bubble.
The winner is the player who has the most fun and can think of the happiest thoughts!**

A version of this game board is on the CD

3. Faces and Feelings

Use these photocopiable outlines of faces for children to draw expressions. Use the words first, and then try without the words.

I'm happy

I'm sad

I'm sleepy

I'm hot

I'm cross

I'm scared

4. One Hundred Square

A 100 square template to use for making up games. You can use it to create games based on the faces on the previous page. For example, players have a counter each and roll dice to move. Even squares are happy, odd squares are sad (you can use other emotions as the game develops). When a player lands they have to draw a face that fits that square. Older children can tell a story that fits.

There are lots of possibilities.

1 00	99	98	97	96	95	94	93	92	91
81	82	83	84	85	86	87	88	89	90
80	79	78	77	76	75	74	73	72	71
61	62	63	64	65	66	67	68	69	70
60	59	58	57	56	55	54	53	52	51
41	42	43	44	45	46	47	48	49	50
40	39	38	37	36	35	34	33	32	31
21	22	23	24	25	26	27	28	29	30
20	19	18	17	16	15	14	13	12	11
1	2	3	4	5	6	7	8	9	10

A version of this game board is on the CD

5. Word Frames

These photocopiable frames are for you to make your own book cards.
They are on the CD as Microsoft Word documents, at full size. Print them, or print
and copy them. Children enjoy colouring them.

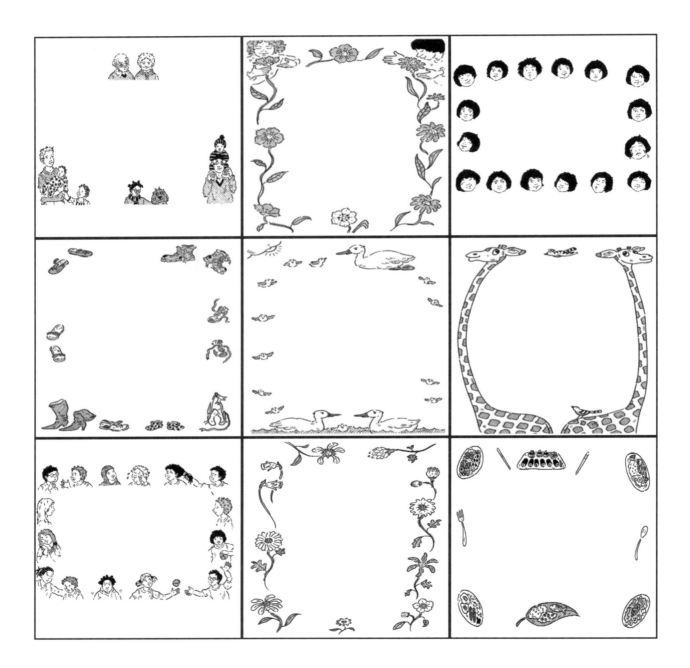

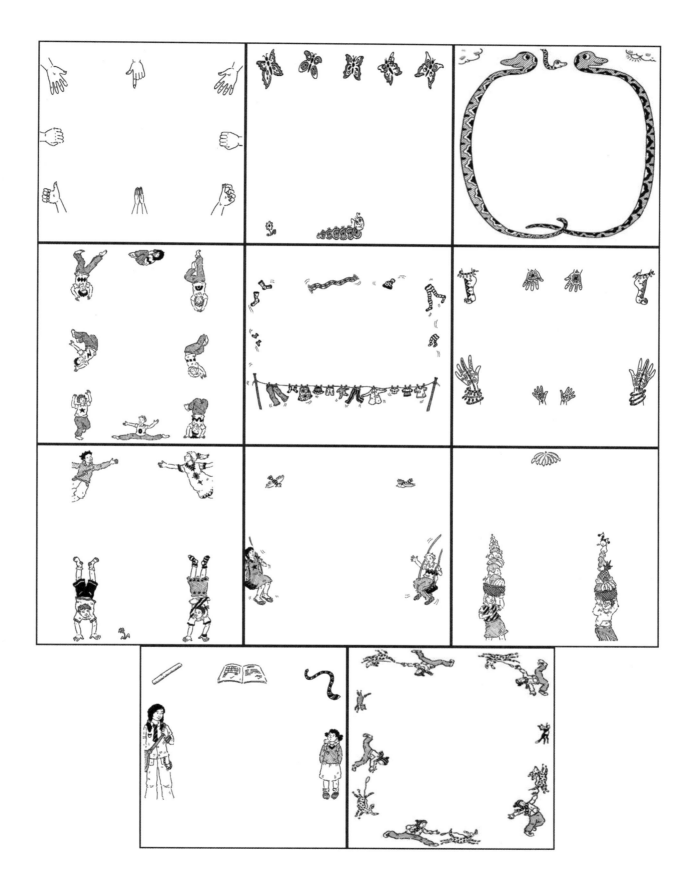

Contents of the CD

The CD which accompanies this book is not for sale.

It is not to be distributed separately from this book. It is protected by the laws of copyright and may not, without the written permission of the publisher, be reproduced, stored or transmitted in any format, including electronically and by means of the internet.

The contents of the CD are licenced for use only by the owner of this book. All rights reserved.

The CD contains the following resources:

1. Emotional Literacy Book List

A list in Microsoft Excel of all the stories listed in this book, together with details of their authors and publishers and the emotions to which they particularly relate.

2. Book Cards

Versions of book cards in Microsoft Word. Each card contains a summary of the story, the emotions and feelings to which it relates and suggestions about how it it might be used to promote discussion.

3. 'I Can' Statements

Colourful display cards for a variety of uses, in Microsoft Word.

4. Word Banks

Lists of words to do with emotions and feelings.

5. Word Frames

Original illustrations for word frames for users to make their own book cards.

6. The Emotional Literacy Kit

Games and activities to encourage children to recognise and talk about emotions.

Appendix

Books grouped according to common themes. See the alphabetical list on pages 28-55 for summaries and descriptions.

Starting school, coping with school, making and following rules

Billy & the Big New School
David Goes to School
Wanda's First Day

Looking after ourselves, healthy eating

Dr Dog
Green Poems
Hair in Funny Places
I Will Not Ever Never Eat a Tomato
I've Got Nits
So Hungry
The World Came to My Place Today

Expressing feelings, empathising

All Kinds of Feelings
Good Days, Bad Days
Hoot & Holler
I Feel Happy
I Love You, Blue Kangaroo
I'm Not Invited
Just Like You
L is for Loving
The Happy Hedgehog
The Polar Bear & the Snow Cloud
The Red Tree
The Three Grumpies
What Colour is Love
Where Are You, Blue Kangaroo
You've Got Gragons

Being proud of what you can do

Zed the Zebra

Acknowledging mistakes and learning from them

Good Baby, Bad Baby
No, David

Stories about love and friendship (continued)

I'll Always Love You
Just Like You
Little Beaver & the Echo
My Friend Bear
No Matter What
Sitting Duck
The Lion Who Wanted to Love
The Rainbow Fish
What Colour is Love

Stories about good manners

Excuse Me!
Kitty Princess & the Newspaper Dress
Rude Mule
Tissue, Please!

Stories about the arrival of young siblings

A Special Something
Baby on Board
Don't Be Horrid, Henry
Little Snail's Big Surprise
Sophie & the New Baby
Truelove

Stories about worrying and anxiety

You've Got Dragons

Stories about death and grieving

Badger's Parting Gifts
Goodbye, Mousie
Up in Heaven

Thinking about what we say and how is affects how others feel

David Goes to School
I'll Always Love You
I'm Sorry
It Was You, Blue Kangaroo
Lilly's Purple Purse
Rude Mule
The Smartest Giant in Town

Thinking about what we do and how is affects how others feel

Badger's Bad Mood
I Love You, Blue Kangaroo

Is That What Friends Do?

Jennifer Jones Won't Leave Me Alone

Princess Snooty-cat

The Rainbow Fish

Three Cheers for Ostrich

Voices in the Park

Willy & Hugh

Being patient

Frong & the Stranger

Embracing each other's similarities and differences

All Kinds of Bodies

All Kinds of People

Giraffes Can't Dance

I'm Special

Lost - one green dog

Martha's Friends

My Friend Bear

My Nose

Who Loves You, Little Beetle?

Willy & Hugh

Co-operating with others

A Cat & a Dog

Rainbow Fish to the Rescue

Helping others who need a friend

Have You Seen Elvis?

Martha's Friends

Willy & Hugh

Taking care of the world and the environment

Five Little Friends

Green Poems

Letters From Around the World

Mole & Baby Bird

One World

The World Came to my Place Today

Being the best you can be; setting goals

A Cultivated Wolf

The Lion Who Wanted to Love

The Very Lazy Ladybird

Willy the Wizard

Wonder Goal
You Choose
Being honest, telling the truth
David Gets into Trouble
Jennifer Jones
The Gossipy Parrot

Showing respect
I Don't Care
Sharing
A Friend for Little Bear
Five Little Friends
Mine
Mouse, Mole & the Falling Star
The Rainbow Fish
The Richest Crocodile in the World
The Smartest Giant in Town
The Selfish Crocodile
Perseverance
A Cultivated Wolf
Big Bird
Billywise
Don't Let Go
Frog is a Hero
Giraffes Can't Dance
Really Brave Tim
Willy the Wizard
War, family separation, asylum
Peter's Song
The Colour of Home

More books about stories and storytelling

Making time for stories ...

Cooking from Stories

Children love these activities, which build on links between simple food preparation and favourite stories. Read the story, then make and try the food.

ISBN 978-1-904187-04-2

Maths from Stories

Lots of stories and rhymes involve numbers and counting. Here is a selection by Neil Griffiths, with tips for making the most of them.

ISBN 978-1-905019-25-0

Puppets in Stories

Puppets are great for getting children talking, thinking and imagining. This book will help you use puppets to enhance both play and storytelling.

ISBN 978-1-905019-33-5

Mary Medlicott is a well known storyteller. She believes that storytelling is a natural human activity and anyone can do it. In these books she shows how.

Cooking Up A Story

... is a wonderful collection of stories and storytelling advice. The book is organised as a menu, with a series of courses offered for developing the imagination. The emphasis is on creativity and enjoyment – getting children engaged and stimulating their thinking. The sound, practical guidance for practitioners will help even the least confident to make the most of storytime. Delightfully illustrated in full colour.

order CUS   ISBN 1-905019-00-9 • 978-1-905019-00-7

The Little Book of Storytelling

... offers expert tips on storytelling to help you build stories around children's own ideas.

More resources for dealing with feelings

Talking about feelings ...

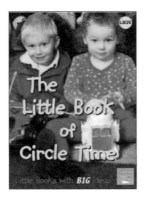

The Little Book of Circle Time

Many practitioners use circle time to get children to explore their thoughts and feelings by putting them into words. This Little Book contains simple, straightforward guidance on introducing, planning and running circle time sessions.

ISBN 978-1-904187-94-3

The Little Book of Persona Dolls

Bullying, name calling, unkindness, misunderstanding are some of the issues tackled here. An experienced teacher gives ideas for using persona dolls to challenge stereotypes and help children to open their minds and understand other people and how they feel.

ISBN 978-1-904187-86-8

Taking notice of other people ...

The Little Book of Listening

Why won't they listen? Here are lots of activities specially devised to encourage attentive listening, taking turns, paying attention to others and concentrating.

ISBN 978-1-904187-69-1